THE KNOT

How to Secure Healthy, Modern Relationships
While Not Being Tied to Marriage's Past

THE KNOT

How to Secure Healthy, Modern Relationships
While Not Being Tied to Marriage's Past

DANA ROBERT HICKS

SacraSage

Nampa, Idaho

Print ISBN 978-1-948609-74-6
Ebook ISBN 978-1-948609-76-0

Printed in the United States of America
Library of Congress Cataloguing-in-Publication Data

The Knot: How to Secure Healthy, Modern Relationships While Not Being Tied to Marriage's Past / Dana Robert Hicks

FOR CHRISTINA

"I knew the second I met you that there was
something about you I needed.
Turns out it wasn't something about you at all.
It was just you."

—JAMIE MCGUIRE, *BEAUTIFUL DISASTER*—

Contents

PREFACE

I Wasn't Supposed to Write this Book

"By all means marry; if you get a good wife,
you'll become happy; if you get a bad
one, you'll become a philosopher."

–SOCRATES–

"I loved her against reason, against promise,
against peace, against hope, against happiness,
against all discouragement that could be."

–CHARLES DICKENS, *GREAT EXPECTATIONS*–

"You gave me a forever within the
numbered days, and I'm grateful."

–JOHN GREEN, *THE FAULT IN OUR STARS*–

MENTAL SOUNDTRACK

Coldplay, "Adventure of a Lifetime"
Gotye, "Somebody That I Used to Know"

Why are so many people miserable in their marriages? Amidst rapid societal change, what is the future of marriage? Does it have one? How can Christians understand marriage in fresh ways that help them to actually navigate the difficulty and joy of marriage in the modern world?

I've read a lot of books on marriage. However, there were very few, if any, that were addressing the changing role of marriage in our world and what that meant for those in the Christian tradition. So, I pitched the idea to a publisher, and they loved it—even agreed to publish it. I initially wanted to write it under a pseudonym because of my own history.

I never thought I would write a book on marriage. But then, as a pastor and teacher with many years of pastoral counseling experience, I realized that I had witnessed and thought about many marriages close up. Like everyone, I understand and experience the world from a particular point of view. For 25 years, I was ordained and served in the Church of the Nazarene—a small Evangelical denomination rooted in the Holiness movement of the early 20th Century. I left that denomination and served with the United Methodist Church for another five years before I retired from pastoral ministry. I wore other hats as well: overseeing a small NGO that did orphan care and economic development projects in Africa, and then training pastors in a graduate program as an adjunct Professor of Missional Leadership. I trained academically not really in marriage or interpersonal relationships, but in theology and leadership.

That's the first reason why initially I didn't think I should be the person to write this book. The second reason? My personal track record with marriage is nothing to brag about. As I would talk to people about the book, I would always take a deep breath before I would explain its ideas and then give a list of disclaimers: "It's not about how to make your marriage better. As if I know anything about THAT!" People would nod and smile politely.

If repetition improves one's ability at a task, it may be my only redeeming quality when it comes to understanding marriage comes from repetition. I've put in my 10,000 hours. I got married for the first time at 23 years old, when she was 21. The State of Idaho barely trusted her enough to buy beer, but gladly issued us a marriage license. I now know that because of our age, statistically, the odds were stacked against us succeeding. But back then all our friends at our Christian college were getting hitched, so it made sense to us. We're bound together for life now because we have three children together, but the marriage ended after 19 years.

Fourteen years after our divorce, we're friends. As I worked on the manuscript of this book, I sent portions to her for feedback. As we discussed some of the ideas in this book, we both agreed that if we had known then what we now know, we might have found a way to keep the marriage moving forward instead of abandoning it. Back then, we didn't know that marriage had any flexibility in it, nor did we have the words and concepts to describe what we were thinking and feeling.

My second marriage lasted nine years. That divorce was, without a doubt, the most painful experience of my life. We are not friends. If you met her, she would have all kinds of awful things to say about me; some likely true, some likely not. In the aftermath of that experience, I decided that marriage was not for me. Remember the saying: "Fool me once, shame on you; fool me twice, shame on me?" My attitude was: never again.

When Christina and I met, in some ways we had a lot in common. In other ways, we were as polar opposites. We both grew up in the Christian tradition but found a spirituality and a God much bigger than the limits of what was prepackaged and marketed to us in our youth. We were both divorced, hated the institution of marriage, and never, ever wanted to be married again. "I don't want to be anyone's *wife*," she would say with disgust in her voice. I found this reassuring because I didn't want to be anyone's husband. I was broken and burned out and I needed her in ways that I did not understand at the time. Christina helped me discover that grace remains an abstract concept until you experience it through another person. Because of her, I am not completely cynical, angry, and bitter today.

We planned on living out our days, unmarried and golfing all the Scottsdale golf courses until we rode off into the Arizona sunset in a golf cart, clubs rattling in the back. We thought Elizabeth Gilbert's book, *Eat. Pray. Love.* would be the compass and guide for what the remainder of our days would look like. But life sometimes takes sudden turns, and when the doctor told her the biopsy was cancer, all the rules changed. She died seven months later on her own terms: just the two of us together in deathly silence alone in our Scottsdale home. I held her hand in our bedroom as she breathed her last breath.

This project came to fruition because of her encouragement with the writing process. I started writing the book as she was recovering from dehumanizing doses of chemotherapy, and I would read portions to her. It also came about because, ironically, Christina made me believe again in what the institution of marriage could be.

My good friend, Dr. Reginald Watson also believed in this project before I did. He provided tremendous encouragement and support. It was through long conversations with Reg that I realized that this project might have legs. Reg was both wise and smart—a winning combination. And he was a "Grammar Nazi" who was able to clean up my sloppy writing. To everyone's surprise, on Memorial Day 2022, Reg suddenly passed away from a heart attack. The world is so much darker without his contagious laughter and joy. Thank you for being such a good friend, Reg.

A few others were very helpful in this process: first I will mention my college roommate—"T.O." Most people call him Thomas Jay Oord, and he's now a well-known Philosopher of Religion. We won intramural championships together (let's go, Existential Pigs!), played in more than one rock band together, argued theology, and he has been a source of friendship, encouragement, and challenge for almost 40 years. When I approached Tom with this crazy idea for a book, he was nothing but encouraging from the very beginning. By the way, if you have read Tom's beautiful theology of love and wondered if it is all abstract theology, I can tell you that he genuinely embodies what it means to love God and others.

Debbie Coutts and Bob Hunter, clergy colleagues/friends, were kind enough to read early drafts and speak the truth in love to me about what was good, what needed work, and what need to be clearer. Debbie patiently endured my requests for feedback and spent way too much time wordsmithing with me the sub-title of this book! Thank you for your help and support!

My lifelong friend Marie Marianiello's brilliance, editorial feedback, and wordplay helped me conceptualize the title and guiding metaphor of this book ("knot", "not", "knotty", "naughty", etc.). Thank you for being such a great friend for so many years!

My good friends Jonathon Foster, Carrie Wester, Jenna Beck, and Stephen Campbell not only supported and encouraged me but also helped give invaluable feedback that made me sound like a much better writer than I actually am.

My former colleague Meredith Messinger came through as always with an amazing cover design. If you are looking for a freelance illustrator and/or designer, check her out: meredith fernillustration.com.

Rebecca Adams took my final draft and filled it with a sea of red ink to make it much more readable. Thank you for all your hard work, Rebecca!

A couple of other logistical/legal notes: all the people referenced in this book are either composite characters of different people I have met in my years of being a pastor, or I have received their permission to tell their story on the condition that I change their names and any identifying information about them.

Unless otherwise indicated, all scripture referenced in this book comes from the New Revised Standard Version of the Bible.

As I have written, I have found different songs running through my head. When you write about love, marriage, heartbreak, adultery, and relationships, lots of popular songs seem to capture the *zeitgeist*. Each chapter of this book begins with an indicator of a couple of the songs that made up my mental soundtrack for that chapter. If you are ambitious, you can even listen to the songs before you read the chapter to get in "the zone." And, yes, I was going through Coldplay and Taylor Swift stages as I wrote.

INTRODUCTION

Marriage is a Wonderful Institution, But Who Wants to Live in an Institution?

"I believe that in the search for the answer lies the answer."

–FRANK LLOYD WRIGHT–

"The chief object of education is not to learn things but to unlearn things."

–G. K. CHESTERTON–

MENTAL SOUNDTRACK

Sting, "Brand New Day"
Coldplay, "The Scientist"

I have a thought experiment I like to do with groups when talking about marriage. I will say to them, "If you were about to board an airplane and the gate agent announced, "We've had some maintenance trouble with this airplane, but I think it's going to be fine. There's a 50/50 chance of landing safely at your destination," would you board the plane? No sane person would. Or, if you went to a sushi restaurant and the server said to you, "Not sure how fresh this fish is. But I wouldn't worry about it—I would say there is a 50/50 chance you won't get food poisoning." Would you eat the sushi?" Very few of us would take that risk.

Yet every year, 62 million people in our country roll the dice, take a chance and get married knowing that their odds of success are approximately 50%.[1] We Americans are a romantic lot. Americans as a percentage marry more often than those in the vast majority of other Western countries. We're the inventers and the exporters of the Romantic Comedy, after all. But we also divorce at higher rates than virtually every other Western country. The divorce rate in the US rose quickly from the 1950s to the 1980s and has held steady since then. So, when a couple celebrates 30, 40, or 50+ years of marriage, we celebrate it because, like a marathon runner, we know it's a grind and that it takes commitment and determination to stay married. When the average adult lived to be 40 years old, pledging, "until death do us part" carried a lot less weight than it does when each partner can expect to live well into their 80s or 90s.[2]

Of course, not getting divorced does not equal a happy marriage. The phenomenon of the "semi-happy marriage" arises as a recurring theme among marriage researchers. These marriages are not violent, abusive, or driven by addictions, but nonetheless carry a low-grade misery to them. Women are particularly prone to suffer through these "semi-happy marriages." Some research shows being married to be good for men's health, but not so much for women. Other, more in depth longitudinal studies show, "not only that marriage has little impact on health or happiness but that any positive effects of marriage are likely attributable to a more positive evaluation of one's life rather than improvement on concrete measures."[3] As we will discover later in this book, a small number have found their way to fulfilling and happy marriages. But many more can identify with Groucho Marx when he so aptly summarized many decades ago, "Marriage is wonderful institution...but who wants to live in an institution?"[4]

Our collective disillusionment with marriage begins in our unwillingness to take the plunge. The Pew Research Center reports that only about half of Americans over age 18 are now married. This represents a decline from 72 percent in 1960.[5] The number has been dropping in all age groups, regardless of the state of the economy. Part of the reason for this shift? People are getting married much later in life than they used to. In 2018, the median age for a first marriage rose to an all-time high of 30 for men and 28 for women.[6] Statistically, most Americans will eventually take the leap and marry, but 14 percent of never-married adults say they don't plan to marry at all.

Brittany is typical of many young adults I spoke with over the years. She told me, "My parents fought all the time, and it was a miserable existence for both of them. Marriage has no appeal to me whatsoever. Why would I put myself through *that?*" An additional 27 percent aren't sure whether marriage is a life choice they would like to make. But it's not just single people; 40% of Americans polled in 2010 said marriage was "becoming obsolete."[7]

Of course, marriage and divorce in the US are not monolithic. Unlike in the 1970s, divorce rates today tie more to economic class than to any other factor. Middle-class couples divorce at only about half the rate of poor and working-class couples. One researcher reflects that marriage in our day is emerging as an elite custom.[8]

While working on my degree at Asbury Theological Seminary, I became close friends with Alex, a Southern Baptist minister from Virginia. Once over lunch, I remember arguing with Alex about a truism, that the divorce rate for those who identified as "Christian" skewed no different than the divorce rate for those who did not. Alex insisted, "In the Bible Belt, people may identify as 'Christian' but they are cultural Christians. They use the moniker, but they really don't go to church or live a Christian lifestyle. Those divorce statistics are skewed because they are including all these cultural Christians in their numbers."

Years later, I realized that I was wrong. It turns out that conservative Protestants have a *higher* divorce rate than the general population. Despite Evangelicals disdain for divorce, the Bible Belt has the highest divorce rate in the country, while progressive-minded Massachusetts has the lowest.[9] In one study, demographers Jennifer Glass and Philip Levchak concluded that how many Evangelical one lives near is actually one of the strongest predictive factors in divorce.[10]

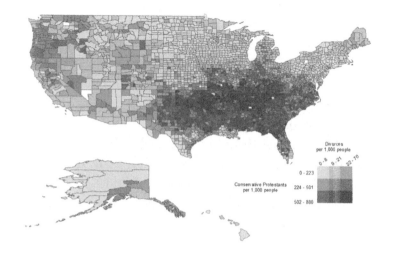

FIGURE 1 – Map of U.S. Counties by Divorce Rate from Jennifer Glass and Philip Levchak, *Red States, Blue States, and Divorce: Understanding the Impact of Conservative Protestantism on Regional Variation in Divorce Rates*

Shortly before my first marriage ended, a parishioner who knew of our troubles paid for us to attend a Mark Gungor *Laugh Your Way to a Better Marriage* seminar.[11] Mark's typical of the Evangelical speaking circuit—his presentation was entertaining, but didn't have a lot of substance. I don't remember much about the seminar except a comment that Mr. Gungor made regarding young men. Mark argued that young men don't grow up and then get married; they get married, become fathers, and then they grow up. Therefore, according to Mr. Gungor, we should encourage young men to marry young so they will grow up quicker.

But in Jennifer Glass and Philip Levchak's research, the distinguishing factor for the increased divorce rates among Evangelicals was not poverty, marriage rates, or domestic violence stemming from patriarchal belief structures. Instead, the researchers concluded, "Restricting sexual activity to marriage and encouraging large families seem to make young people start families earlier in life, even though that may not be best for the long-term survival of those marriages."[12]

There's a common understanding among clergy that we sometimes joke about: nobody calls their pastor and says, "I just wanted to let you know that everything is going great here in our house!" Instead, we often find ourselves with front-row seats to some of people's biggest life crises. And no place is closer and more intimate than the view we have of people's marriages. Like anyone who has been in this business for any length of time, I've seen it all: the cheaters, the bored, the abusive, the swingers, those struggling with their sexual-identity, the burned-out, the lazy, the polyamorous—the list is endless. Sometimes I feel like the Farmers Insurance commercials—"I know a thing or two because I've seen a thing or two."

For as many stories as I've seen, there are an equal number of different endings. Some people can rise to the occasion of whatever crisis they face and evolve into a new form of marriage that proves healthier and stronger than the previous one. Others, for a myriad of reasons, can't navigate the challenges and they decided that the best of a bunch of bad options would be to call it quits on the marriage.

The gut response for many when faced with the divorce rate can be judgmental: I think of the grumpy old pastors at pastor's retreat who lament, "those darn lazy kids don't know how to honor a commitment when things get tough." But it's not that simple. If a process or an institution fails at its desired outcome more often than it succeeds, it might be time to look at the process or the institution itself, rather than the character of the individuals involved. Remember the old saying in organizational management, "Every system is perfectly designed to get the results that it gets."[13]

A few years ago, I read a book at the recommendation from a colleague by Stephanie Coontz, an historian from Evergreen College in Olympia, Washington. Her book began a process of me re-thinking everything I thought I knew about marriage. She pointed out that marriage, as we understand it today, did not evolve in a vacuum. Social, religious, philosophical, and political forces shaped how the system came to be designed. Some of these forces are good and some not so good. The more I delved into the research and read the history of the institution of marriage, the more I became convinced that perhaps divorce rates are not as much a crisis of character as a systemic crisis.

I got to thinking about romantic love, and how we assume it's the basis for a good marriage. Now romantic love is love, sure. But isn't romantic love qualitatively different than the love that we have for our children, our parents, and our pets? While we may bond with other beings and care for their overall well-being, the chemical reactions that we experience and romantic love's distinctive social role makes it unique among love's many expressions.

I know as I write these words that it'll be an uphill battle to get people to change how they think about romantic love and marriage. It's impossible to talk about romantic love without our own emotional biases getting in the way—we're all biased and personally invested in our ideas and experiences of love. We all have our own unique experiences. Nobody reading this book comes with a "view from nowhere."

I've found that many people's knee-jerk reaction to re-thinking or changing romantic love and marriage assumes the alternative must be the promotion of a world in which "love has been eliminated and replaced by constant, guilt-free sex."[14] Some of this reaction comes from the political divide we live in and divisive discussions surrounding love and sex. Some people try to minimize the legitimacy of a relationship by saying it is "just sex." Or others try to make a coupling more legitimate by calling it "true love." But while love and sex aren't the same thing, they're certainly not competitors. We shouldn't diss love, nor sex either. People who find themselves outside of social norms often find themselves on the receiving end of collective indifference that makes them invisible. Many have had family members tell them that their relationship isn't love at all, but only lust or confusion.

Reading Jonathan Haidt's landmark book *The Righteous Mind* has helped me understand the psychology of moral reasoning and see how some of you may receive this book. Haidt argues that moral intuitions come to us first and then our minds find ways to logically justify those intuitions.[15] As such, some of the content of this book may be triggering to your moral intuitions and you will find it difficult to reason your way out of those intuitions. However, if you have *already* experienced some cognitive dissonance surrounding romantic love and marriage, this book will give you some tools to help reflect on your experiences theologically and practically. Similar to a cognitive behavioral approach, I am guessing that if you don't like the way you are feeling about romantic love and marriage, perhaps me helping you change the way you are thinking will allow your feelings to follow your thoughts.

On a societal level, social change can be painfully slow. Yet many have been surprised at how quickly things can move when society hits a tipping point. Interracial marriage and gay marriage provide good examples of deep change from recent history. So maybe marriage can change somewhat and still retain its essence. Just as humans can change their clothing or their feelings about spaghetti squash and remain the same person, social constructs such as marriage can adjust while keeping their essence. For example, this Spring, Major League Baseball announced that the National League would now also use the Designated Hitter rule. Baseball is a social construct. It's what it is because we agree to what the rules and traditions are going to be. Even though the DH rule changed in the National League, we still have baseball—to the dismay of some baseball purists.

Sometimes biological forces within some human beings war against the social constructs we create. Like so much of human behavior, when you suppress the expression of emotions in one area such as marriage or relationships, it tends to express itself in another area. Those ensuing expressions often aren't very healthy or helpful. The catastrophe surrounding gay conversion therapy gives a good case-in-point—some things are changeable, and some things are hard-wired in us. No amount of social pressure will switch off queer people's neurochemical love responses to same-sex partners. In the words of the philosopher/poet Taylor Swift, "Shade never made anybody less gay."[16] Biology sometimes forces us to reexamine our social constructs.

In the pages that follow I hope you will be able to appreciate both the beauty and the plasticity of the social construct we call marriage. I believe that a fresh look at how the institution of marriage got to where it is today can help us re-imagine marriage in a way that is healthier for ourselves, our partners, and our communities.

This book aims to discuss in an accessible, caring way the history, patterns and research I've discovered about marriage.

It's not an academic treatise, but neither is it just a collection of anecdotes. I'm not a professional expert, but I've learned from failure and professionally counselled many people, whose experiences you might find useful. I'm not going to tell you in an easy quick-fix how to be happily married: rather, this book attempts to think out loud about what I've observed in others as well as in my own journey in the experience of marriage. I intend it to start a conversation, not be a sermon or a monologue. When it comes to the future of marriage, the stakes are high, and we desperately need to have this conversation. I hope to give people a framework to think theologically and ethically about their marriages, and my wish is to give them the freedom to explore new expressions of their love. So, as you read these pages, please don't be a passive observer but feel free to push back, challenge, question, and take these thoughts further than I could have ever imagined.

CHAPTER 1

Trapped in History

"People are trapped in history and
history is trapped in them."

–JAMES BALDWIN–

"There's this package of traditions and expectations
that we've bundled together and labeled 'romantic
love,' and it gives our society a certain structure.
But as soon as we know a little history, sociology,
or cultural anthropology, we see clearly that this
isn't the only way a society may organize itself."

–CARRIE JENKINS–

MENTAL SOUNDTRACK

Bruce Hornsby and The Range, "The Way It Is"
Tina Turner, "What's Love Got to Do with It?"

In 2003, while pastoring a church I started in Tucson, Arizona, I preached a series of sermons called *From Ozzie to Ozzy*. In this sermon series I juxtaposed the iconic 1950s TV series *Ozzie and Harriet* with the then popular reality TV show, *The Osbournes,* starring rock legend Ozzy Osbourne and his family. It was a way to recognize how much marriage and family had changed over the previous fifty years. My purpose was to call people back to what I understood at the time as a more "traditional" understanding of marriage and family.

It has taken me two decades of learning and un-learning to come face to face with this reality: there is no such thing as "traditional" marriage. In fact, marriage has expressed itself in such infinitely diverse ways over the eons and in different parts of the world that the term "marriage" almost defies definition. In some societies, husbands and wives live apart. In other places, they don't share financial resources or child-rearing responsibilities. Of the 1,231 cultures recorded in the Ethnographic Atlas Codebook, 85% of them practice polygamy. Marriages have functioned in myriad forms for human beings.

During my first trip to Africa to train pastors, I was surprised to find polygamy practiced among many church leaders. When one African pastor noticed my surprise, he told me, "You Americans practice polygamy also. You are just married to one wife at a time rather than several at once."

Like my church members in Tucson in 2003, most culture warriors who pine for the golden age of marriage look to the decade of the 1950s as their model. But perception and reality carry much more nuance than what first meets the eye. Until 250 years ago, the idea that love should be the foundation for marriage, or that hormone-filled young people should be the ones to make the important decision about who their life partner was to be, were considered absurd. Marriage was far too economically and politically important for that.

Of course, always bubbling below the surface in the history of marriage lurks the issue of gender: gender roles, expectations, power, and control. But if one were to try to find a common thread for "marriage" throughout history in various cultures, we could argue that people have married for one primary reason: survival. Sometimes this meant survival of the husband and/or wife; more commonly it also meant the survival of progeny, extended family, and in-laws.

Today, marriage has very little, if anything, to do with the greater community or with extended families. In reference to planning for one's wedding day, the tagline for the website TheKnot.com proclaims, "Welcome to your day, your way." Offered up are page after page of how to make your wedding "totally you." From an historical perspective, we can't over-emphasize enough how much this mindset makes a hard-turn from at least 3,000 years of marriage history. It's true that people have fallen in love throughout human history, sometimes even with their spouses. But while we certainly can connect love and marriage, historically speaking, marriage was not primarily about love—it was about practicality and survival.

As a result, most of what historically we have called "marriage" correlates very little to how we understand love and marriage today. For much of human history, people had no choice about whom they married or whether to have children. Men ruled over their families and legally owned a wife's property, earnings, sexuality, and sometimes her very self. The consequences for children born out of wedlock were minimal for men but devastating for women. It was the institution of marriage, not government, that conferred on people the rights of jobs, education, and property. Most people today will agree that many of these "traditional" aspects of marriage we should leave in the waste bins of history.

Marriage Before the Agricultural Revolution

As a child I watched The Flintstones animated cartoon and assumed that pre-historic humanity must be very similar to 1950s households, except for a few modern appliances. Apparently, many anthropologists in the 1970s also watched The Flintstones, because until very recently, anthropologists assumed domestic life before the agricultural revolution was a lot like *Leave it to Beaver* or *Ozzie and Harriet.* More recent and credible research, however, shows that the domestic life of our hunter-gatherer ancestors more resembled our bonobo primate cousins than that of modern humans.[1] By observing current pre-modern tribes, we discovered that prehistoric men and women had to be much more cooperative with the village in order to survive. Our modern competitive zero-sum mindset often assumes an "us" versus "them" mentality. But rather than perceiving that an advantage for someone else must be an equivalent loss for us, the entire prehistoric family had to collaboratively provide for the whole tribe. Even reproduction was a group project.[2]

We tend to think that biological influences surrounding romantic love that we experience today are just natural and uncomplicated. But they come from a complex cultural system that evolved for the promotion of social bonding and cooperation. Processes of biological and cultural evolution, looked at honestly, are not very romantic and not at all concerned with our happiness. Rather, evolution focuses on finding the most effective strategy for the survival of our genes.[3]

Once *homo sapiens* figured out if you plant a seed in the ground, it will grow into a plant, life began to change dramatically for us. No longer did people have to rely on stalking prey and gathering berries. Now, they could focus on crops and stay in one place. Suddenly, survival was much easier:

> As societies learned to produce, store, and distribute food, they developed the characteristics of modern civilizations: densely populated cities, centralized government, organized religion, private property, specialized occupations, public works, taxation, technology, and science. People lived as hunter-gatherers for tens of thousands of years before they began to plant crops and domesticate animals. Once this happened, however, the transition to modern civilization was rapid and fundamental.[4]

But this transition into the agricultural revolution didn't necessarily improve our ancestors' lives when it came to things like health and happiness. In fact, anthropologist Jared Diamond has called the agricultural revolution "a catastrophe from which we have never recovered" and "the worst mistake in the history of the human race."[5] Food no longer functioned just a means of survival but as a pathway to wealth. Suddenly, cooperation was no longer the norm; rather, competition between neighbors for resources, and questions about who owned what, rose to the surface. Our ancestors began to see the world in terms of "ownership" and "property."

Anthropologist Agustin Fuentes notes that one study of forty-six meta-analyses demonstrated that there are only a handful of gender traits that are consistent across cultures. One of those traits is the physiological upper-body strength of men in comparison to their female counterparts. Consequently, men in this new world had an advantage over women when it came to plough-farming. Since plough-farming was incompatible with childcare, the division of labor roles quickly evolved with men doing the field work and women relegated to child-rearing and household work.[6] Without control over food, women devolved into second-class citizens. Children became no longer an extra burden, but instead viewed as even more potential workers for the field and thus added prosperity. In this new world concerns arose over how to keep unscrupulous men from taking women for themselves, and how to ensure that men's property and wealth would be passed on to their progeny. With all this began a brand-new institution: marriage.

Yet, in much the same way we pine for the "good ol' days," oral tradition from our ancient ancestors reveals a longing for the "good ol' days" of men wandering about looking for food and not having to do the hard work of farming. While the agricultural revolution prospered the human race, it came with a social and cultural price.

Marriage in the Hebrew Scriptures

Against this backdrop, we can look at the Hebrew scriptures and the values it develops. In the very first book of the Bible, we find Adam and Eve as hunter-gatherers in a garden. Crisis ensues as the prototypical woman (Eve) tempts the prototypical man (Adam) away from hunting for food toward the "womanly" work of gathering by giving him the knowledge of what is "good" and "bad" (or, edible and poisonous) in the Garden. For an ancient people, this narrative provided an explanation for why men would rule over women, why women would be dependent on men, and why men were cursed to work so hard tilling the ground.[7]

For the Ancient Hebrews, love, marriage, and divorce often reflected their ancient world's ethos. Even before Abraham had his first descendent, something called the Hammurabi Code governed the ancient world. According to this Code, a husband could divorce a wife at any time and for any reason, simply by walking out of the house. Women at this time in history could be abandoned and stuck with raising children as a single parent. If a woman had sons and found some way to raise them, these young men might get old enough to work the farm and turn a profit. However, the ex-husband could return anytime he wanted to, reclaiming the ex-wife, the kids, the money, and the farm. In practical terms, the Code implied if a wife were abandoned by her husband, she could theoretically remarry; however, in practice men knew that the first husband could be lurking around out there somewhere, coming back at any time to reclaim her. Consequently, the ancient Code skewed very much in favor of men and left women and their fortunes very vulnerable.

While marriage among the Ancient Hebrews was much more progressive than other ancient cultures, the Law still considered women property and they had virtually no more rights than slaves. Often, marriages were arranged for the purpose of providing a bond between families. While there may have been some exceptions to this, most of these arranged marriages would have had little, if anything, to do with romantic love as we understand it today. We can see this by understanding the so-called Levirate marriage, which was such a major practice for the Ancient Hebrews. If a woman had not borne a son and became a widow, her late husband's brother needed to marry her unless he went through an elaborate ritual with the town elders.[8] The practice of Levirate marriage helped preserve the loss of family property in case a woman was tempted to marry outside the clan, and it helped to carry on the existing family bloodline.

We have here a patriarchal world. A man who committed adultery did not commit a wrongful act against his own wife, but against his male neighbor, whose property the mistress was. A woman could be stoned for not being able to prove her virginity before a marriage.[9] A woman could be forced to marry her rapist.[10] Some cultures today still bear traces of these ancient mores and practices.

Like many cultures in human history, non-monogamous forms of marriage like polygamy show up very commonly in Ancient Israel and were practiced by many biblical men: Abraham, Ahab, Belshazzar, Caleb, David, Esau, Ezra, Hosea, Jacob, Manasseh, Moses, Nahor, Rehoboam, Saul, Simeon, and Solomon, to name a few. Concubines were commonplace as either second-tier wives or mistresses with whom wealthier men found pleasure. In our modern vernacular, we would call these men with concubines "sugar daddies."

The Old Testament scholar Walter Brueggemann reminds us that, "the Bible does not speak with a single voice on any topic. Inspired by God as it is, all sorts of persons have a say in the complexity of Scripture, and we are under mandate to listen, as best we can, to all of its voices."[11] Dr. Brueggemann's many-voiced observation is especially true of love, marriage, and sex in the Hebrew scriptures. We see sex in the Hebrew Bible sometimes valued as a path for connection, bonding, and pleasure. But this kind of sexual connection didn't necessarily happen in the framework of marriage, as the unmarried couple in the Song of Solomon demonstrates.[12]

From our contemporary point-of-view, the ancient world was not a good time to be a woman generally, or a married woman specifically. People in the Hebrew Bible treated sex and marriage as transactional and very different than the way it's understood in most religious institutions today. So when culture warriors pine for a return to "biblical marriage," I'm often perplexed by what they mean.[13]

Divorce in Ancient Israel

Compared to the law of other ancient cultures, the Hebrew scriptures remarkably show relative love and concern for women. If a marriage did break up in Ancient Israel, Deuteronomy provided for a "certificate": "Suppose a man enters into marriage with a woman, but she does not please him because he finds something objectionable about her, and so he writes her a certificate of divorce, puts it in her hand, and sends her out of his house...."[14] The "certificate" protected the woman, because it meant the first husband could never come back and reclaim her. Therefore she had some rights, compared to the ancient Code in surrounding cultures.

In this same passage, Deuteronomy mentions grounds for divorce because "she does not please him because he finds something objectionable about her..." In the Hebrew, it literally reads, "finds some uncleanness about her." Most Rabbis interpreted this to mean sexual unfaithfulness. In other cases, Rabbis understood that there were provisions for divorce because of abuse and abandonment. In Exodus 21, the law concerns itself with polygamous relationships and the dynamics that happened when a man took on a second wife. Predictably, some men would lose interest and neglect their first wife, so the law read: "If he takes another wife to himself, he shall not diminish the food, clothing, or marital rights of the first wife. And if he does not do these three things for her, she shall go out without debt, without payment of money."[15] Again, the law sought to protect women by allowing a provision for them to get a "certificate" to remarry after divorce.

For the ancient rabbis, these two passages became the classic texts in the Hebrew Scriptures governing divorce. From these texts, rabbis concluded that the vows of marriage involved three things: 1) Fidelity–to be faithful (Deuteronomy 24); 2) Provision–food, clothing, housing, etc. (Exodus 21); and 3) Sexual intimacy and affection. If a spouse broke these rules, the victim of the broken vows had a right to get divorced whether they were male or female. Moreover, the "certificate" ensured that there was no such thing as a divorce that did not include the right to remarry.

Rabbis loved to debate, and they would often debate what exactly constituted the breaking of these vows. How much food was included in that promise? What about clothing? How about conjugal love? Some rabbis came up with rules around physical intimacy. For example, the husband had to offer to be physically intimate with his wife at least twice a week, or she had the right to divorce him. The Rabbis made exceptions to this rule for some cases. For instance, if the husband were a donkey driver, he only had to offer physical intimacy one time a week. Perhaps in our day it would compare to being a trucker out on the road.[16] Rabbis also recognized that abandonment was an extreme form of breaking the vow to provide, and abuse was an extreme form of breaking the vow to sexual intimacy and affection, and both were therefore grounds for divorce.

Divorce is difficult and heartbreaking—then and now. The Hebrew Scriptures set up ways to prevent worse injustice and suffering when the marriage vows were broken. At least three things made the ancient Hebrews unique and progressive when it came to understanding domestic relations in the ancient world:

1) Women had rights
2) The Rabbis recognized abandonment and abuse as grounds for divorce
3) Marriage began to be thought of as something more than merely a way to survive or to pass on wealth to descendants

Hillel and Shammai were two of the most famous and in-fluential rabbis who lived not long before Jesus and who dominated rabbinic teaching. Hillel reflected on Deuteronomy 24:1 in which Moses says a man can divorce his wife for "a cause of sexual immorality" and gave this interpretation: that Moses *could* have said that a man could divorce his wife "for sexual immorality," but Moses includes this phrase: "for the *cause* of sexual immorality." Hillel reasoned that this word must refer to another cause, a different ground for divorce beside sexual immorality. Since it was just the word *cause*, Hillel concluded that it must mean *any cause*. In other words, Hillel said that

Deuteronomy 24 meant that a man could divorce his wife for two reasons: sexual immorality or *any* cause.

Of course, Hillel, like all rabbis, was a man. Hillel concluded that this "any cause" divorce should be available only to men. This "cause" covered just about any fault one could conceive, and rabbis would joyfully list different faults they believed a husband could divorce his wife for under this "any cause" provision. These included if a wife spoiled her husband's dinner, if she walked around with her hair improperly unbound, if she argued in a voice loud enough to be heard in the next house, and so forth.

The "any cause" divorce had the drawback of being more expensive. If the husband could prove that a spouse had committed adultery or abuse in court, then a husband would not have to pay a *ketubah*—the marriage inheritance that was promised at the wedding. If a husband got an "any cause" divorce, then he had to pay that inheritance. Nevertheless, not long after Hillel introduced this new teaching, "any cause" divorce became the most popular form of divorce in Israel.

One can see the implications of Hillel's teachings in the opening of the New Testament. In Matthew's Gospel, Joseph finds out Mary is pregnant with a child not his. Matthew records, "Her husband Joseph, being a righteous man and unwilling to expose her to public disgrace, planned to dismiss her quietly."[17] The word "quietly" here reflects not just a vague adjective, but a technical term. Joseph decided was he would not take Mary to court and prove that she was guilty of adultery, which would have let him off the hook for the marriage inheritance promise. Rather, he decided to get an "any cause" divorce—ala Hillel—which required no proof of adultery. This meant that Joseph would have to swallow the financial cost and support the child.

But Rabbi Shammai promoted another school of thought surrounding divorce in Ancient Israel: Shammai fell in line with the historical teaching of the rabbis of the past and disagreed with Hillel. Shammai argued that Deuteronomy 24:1 refers *only* to divorce being allowed for sexual immorality, not for "any cause." Hillel fell in line with the traditional rabbinic teaching of divorce being admissible on the basis of Exodus 21, when one of the partners had broken the vow for provision, or the vow for affection. Where the two rabbis differed was their interpretation of Deuteronomy 24: was an "any cause" divorce legitimate?

As the New Testament begins, we can see one of the big debates of the day between the followers of Hillel and the followers of Shammai. Everyone thought this grounds for divorce question was relevant and important, and many saw it as a question over the future of marriage.

Marriage and Divorce in the New Testament

Although as far as we know Jesus never married or had children (a radical life choice for a rabbi in his day), he brought a sweeping new understanding to marriage that stood in contrast to the broader culture. Jesus did *not* stress marriage and family as being of primary importance. Instead, he taught that God and his movement in human history was a higher calling. Belonging to Jesus' radical new community had nothing to do with birth, class, tribe, geography, ethnicity, or membership in a nation-state, but instead focused on the coming Kingdom of God, something that was available to all.

Jesus' disciples lamented about his harsh teaching about divorce, saying maybe it'd be easier not to marry in the first place. Jesus didn't disagree with that, hinting that for the sake of the Kingdom of God, some should consider living like a eunuch.[18] When a potential disciple inquired if he might bury his dead father (see to his obligations to his father until the father died) before joining Jesus' movement, Jesus scoffs, "Leave the dead to bury their own dead."[19] When told that his mother and brothers were waiting to see him, Jesus dismissed their request by saying, "My mother and my brothers are those who hear the word of God and do it."[20] In John's Gospel, when the dying Jesus on the cross sees his mother in the crowd with her sister and brother-in-law, Jesus does not commend her to the care of her biological family, but creates a new family for her that transcended DNA. Calling forth John, Jesus says to his mother, "Woman, behold your son," and to the disciple, "Behold your mother."[21] At one point Jesus even said to the crowds, "If you want to be my disciple, you must, by comparison, hate everyone else—your father and mother, wife and children, brothers and sisters—yes, even your own life. Otherwise, you cannot be my disciple."[22] Over and over Jesus emphasized the priority of the Kingdom of God over everything else—including family. Jesus likens it to a pearl of great value, or a treasure hidden in a field that one would sacrifice anything, even family, to possess.[23]

A good number of what few teachings we have from Jesus surrounding marriage come from other people trying to trap or trick Jesus. Jesus did not seem too interested in dealing with these debates. On one occasion, Matthew records that "Some Pharisees came to him, and to test him they asked, 'Is it lawful for a man to divorce his wife for any cause?'"[24] What the Pharisees ask Jesus here doesn't translate into what many have understood this question to be. They're not asking Jesus if divorce is always against the law. Following the Hebrew Scriptures was not open to debate in ancient Israel and divorce was already a part of the law that Moses established. Rather, they're asking for Jesus to weigh in on the Hillel and Shammai debate discussed earlier in this chapter. In other words, how do you interpret Deuteronomy 24? Do you believe in "any cause" divorce?

They don't ask this question sincerely. Matthew indicates that the Pharisees came to trap him. In that day, Herod Antipas ruled Galilee, and Herod Antipas had been married but fell in love with another woman, Herodias. Unfortunately, Herodias

FIGURE 2 – "John the Baptist Reproving Herod" by John Rogers Herbert.

(Herod Antipas' father was Herod the Great who had 43 children by 10 or 11 wives. Herodias was the daughter of one of Herod Antipas' half-brothers. So, this was a real Jerry Springer moment—once they married, Herodias became his wife, his niece, and his sister-in-law. If they had children, Herodias will be their mother, their aunt, and their cousin.)

was also married—to Herod Antipas' brother. So, Herod Antipas got a divorce from his first wife, and he talked Herodias into divorcing his brother so he could marry her. John the Baptist heard about this and confronted Herod Antipas about it. As it turns out, Herod Antipas got a Hillel "any cause" divorce. So, John the Baptist, showing where he stood in the Hillel and Shammai controversy, said to Herod Antipas, "It is not lawful for you to have your brother's wife."[25] Herod Antipas did not take kindly to this interpretation of Deuteronomy 24 and shortly thereafter had John the Baptist executed. So, the question brought to Jesus about "any cause" divorce was *not* innocent. It was disingenuous and meant to be a powder keg. They were trying to get Jesus to commit suicide by Roman ruler.

Jesus nonetheless plays along, recognizing the Hebrew scripture's teaching on divorce as legitimate and that, regrettably, sometimes divorce may be the best of a bunch of bad options. Human beings have a tendency to harden their hearts, Jesus reminds us.[26] Then, addressing the question of "any cause" divorce directly, he says, "And I say to you, whoever divorces his wife, except for sexual immorality, and marries another commits adultery."[27] In other words, he's saying, "I'm a Shammai guy. I'm against 'any cause' divorce."

Because Jesus mentions sexual immorality here as the only ground, some people have thought the New Testament takes the position that the only Biblical grounds for divorce—or for divorce and remarriage—is adultery. This misinterpretation has caused much anguish, heartbreak, and confusion. Growing up in a church that misunderstood this teaching of Jesus, I remember one perplexed woman saying in exasperation, "You mean that if my husband beats me, beats our children, is addicted to drugs and alcohol, steals money, tries to kill me, I have to stay married to him, but if he strays one time sexually, then I can get a divorce?"

To be clear, in Matthew 19 Jesus doesn't invoke the whole Jewish framework of marriage and divorce that was a part of his world as a rabbi. He does not discuss what happens when the vows of Exodus 21 (provision and love) are broken. Jesus addresses only the Hillel/Shammai debate, and first-century listeners would have recognized this. A similar situation in our day would be if someone asked, "Do you think it's OK for a sixteen-year-old to drink?" We automatically supply the words "drink alcohol," because we understand the broader context of what that question means. First-century listeners understood the raging Hillel and Shammai debate and wanted to know where various people stood on their interpretation of Deuteronomy 24:1. But Jesus would have shared the understanding that where people have broken the vows of marriage (Deuteronomy 24:1 and Exodus 21) *and* where they are hardhearted, then divorce may well be the best choice for the people involved. Jesus doesn't say what some people think he does because they don't understand the broader cultural context.

Beyond this one teaching on divorce, Jesus and the writers of the New Testament have surprisingly little to say about marriage. While they had a lot to say about human relationships and what it means to love other people, the *form* of marriage gets very little attention. Paul, like Jesus, did not take a wife and encouraged single fellas to do the same.[28] In fact, in the one New Testament passage where Paul addresses most specifically the *form* a marriage should take, he concedes that it's his opinion only and should not be taken as a divine directive.[29]

In Paul's letter to the Ephesians, he reiterates the Hebrew scripture's view that wives should be subject to their husbands in the same way that slaves should obey their masters and children should obey their parents.[30] His view may not be easy for our modern sensibilities to hear. But to be fair to Paul, he later plants the seeds not just for female equality, but also for the prohibition of slavery that will explode centuries later—"So in Christ Jesus you are all children of God through faith, for all of you who were baptized into Christ have clothed yourselves with Christ. There is neither Jew nor Gentile, neither slave nor free, nor is there male and female, for you are all one in Christ Jesus."[31]

Re-reading every passage in the New Testament that refers to marriage, I've been struck by how dismissive Jesus seems to be about the institution of marriage in comparison to many of his followers today. Part of Jesus' brilliance lay in his ability to reframe questions to focus on human well-being, and not just the preservation of forms and structures. "The Sabbath was made for humankind, and not humankind for the Sabbath,"[32] he would say. Jesus constantly pushed people to see past the superficial layer of meaning in their life circumstances and to examine the deeper questions of the human heart—what it meant to love.

Marriage During the First Seventeen Centuries of Church History

Early Christians followed Jesus and Paul's example; while marriage happened within their culture, it was not held in particularly high esteem. In the spirit of Paul, one early Christian author, Tertullian (150-240), promoted celibacy for disciples of Jesus (although he was married himself). Tertullian pronounced upon marriage negatively as involving the "commixture of the flesh" and that which "consists of that which is the essence of fornication."[33]

By the end of the fourth century, celibacy was venerated. In fact, the idea that marriage was just as worthy a state as celibacy was ruled a heresy.[34] The theologian Augustine of Hippo (354-430), (who was such a womanizer that he was known to pray, "Give me chastity; but not yet!"),[35] declared: "It is better for human society itself not to have need of marriage."[36] While today the Roman Catholic Church recognizes marriage as a sacrament of grace, this was a relatively late development in church history, happening only in 1215 AD. This may be surprising to some who venerate "Christian marriage" over all other ways of life.

For most of the Medieval period in Europe, marriage slowly became more and more institutionalized and monogamous. (Polygamy, the form of marriage taken by the patriarchs, fell away.) However, note that medieval marriages did not become monogamous sexually. Nobles would marry for proprietary concerns but had mistresses on the side. What in our modern vernacular we call "cheating" they called "love." And although they valued or at least tolerated "love," children of mistresses had no legal or social standing; only children of wives had rights.[37]

Following the Reformation in 1517, both the Roman Catholic Church and the upstart Protestants began to slowly give attention to marital harmony and even talked a little about love within marriage. The seeds had been planted for the way we now understand marriage as being based on love. But it would often be two steps forward and one step back. In 1563, the Council of Trent declared: "If anyone says that the married state excels the state of virginity...let him be anathema."[38]

Until this point in human history, marriage had been simply an agreement acknowledged by the extended families. Marriage primarily signaled the coming together of families, not the coming together of two people. As such, parents and friends collaborated to put a marriage together based on very practical considerations. And since marriage was primarily understood to be a contract, not a relationship, love within marriage was seen as troublesome.

Around the Reformation, marriage began to become more recognizable to 21st century people: the law now prohibited polygamy in Europe and the church, and the state began to get involved with the institution of marriage. Churches by no means had a monopoly on marriage, even then. Martin Luther viewed marriage as a "worldly matter" and thought that marriage records should be managed by the state and not the church. The Catholic Church did not require marriages to be officiated by a priest until 1563, and the Church of England did not make it a requirement until 1753. Again, these facts may surprise those invested in modern ideas of traditional marriage, especially within churches.

Marriage had not changed much from ancient times and the advent of the agricultural revolution until the 18th century. But beginning in the 18th century, a seismic shift began to be felt in the way people understood marriage, a shift that would change both the form and function of marriage—for the worse.

CHAPTER 2

The Disney Princess/Rom-Com Industrial Complex: The Rise of Romantic Marriage

"The constraints imposed by social facts are invisible to us, unless we actively try to resist them."

−EMILE DURKHEIM−

"Mawage.
Mawage is wot bwings us togeder today.
Mawage, that bwessed awangment,
that dweam wifin a dweam..."

−THE IMPRESSIVE CLERGYMAN IN *THE PRINCESS BRIDE*−

MENTAL SOUNDTRACK

Frank Sinatra, "Love and Marriage"
Beyoncé, "Single Ladies (Put a Ring on It)"

In the late 18th century, several forces came to play that began to erode the way human beings had understood marriage since the beginning of human history. Wage labor became common in Europe which, in turn, allowed young people to be much less reliant on their parents and extended family for financial support. For young men, this financial independence meant they could make marriage decisions, rather than conferring with parents and extended family. For young women, this meant they could work to earn their own dowry, which freed them from family dependence. About the same time apprenticeships diminished. This meant a shift away from a young man marrying only after he had acquired a skill; now he could marry when he had acquired an income.[1]

It wasn't just sociological shifts—there were shifting intellectual movements as well. Philosophers like John Locke, Nicolas de Condorcet, and Mary Wollstonecraft began to call for equality within marriage and marriage based on love. It's interesting to note, however, that church leaders in that day pushed back against this trend, thinking it was too dangerous to let young people pick their own partners. Nevertheless, by the end of the century, Sweden, Prussia, France, and Denmark had legalized divorce for reasons of incompatibility.[2]

Personal choice slowly entered the arena of picking potential marriage partners and most people were now choosing to marry for romantic love. Marriage was, for the first time in human history, a private relationship rather than a link in a larger alliance of political and economic systems.[3] As a result, the success of a marriage was not measured by the procurement of a big financial settlement, how many children were produced, or how many useful in-laws were acquired; rather, success was measured by the emotional needs of the individual members of the marriage.

The cultural yearning for romantic-based marriages continued to gain momentum throughout the 19th century, reaching its zenith in the 1950s. Male dominance and long-held ideas of women's purity and proper sphere intersected to make the male breadwinner and female homemaker marriage the majority of marriages for the first time in human history. This decade was anything but the historical norm. Stephanie Coontz's well-researched *Marriage, a History* encapsulates this moment in time well:

> The long decade of the 1950s, stretching from 1947 to the early 1960s in the United States…was a unique moment in the history of marriage. Never before had so many people shared the experience of courting their own mates, getting married at will, and setting up their own households. Never had married couples been so independent of extended family ties and community groups. And never before had so many people agreed that only one kind of family was "normal."
>
> The cultural consensus that everyone should marry and form a male breadwinner family was like a steamroller that crushed every alternative view. By the end of the 1950s even people who had grown up in completely different family systems had come to believe that universal marriage at a young age into a male breadwinner family was the traditional and permanent form of marriage.[4]

In many ways, the romantic marriage ideal endures into the 21st Century; Romantic Comedies earn hundreds of millions of dollars a year selling the romantic marriage trope. The enculturation begins with young children being taught to sing with all the marketing genius that the Disney™ Corporation can muster:

> *Someday my prince will come*
> *Someday we'll meet again*
> *And away to his castle we'll go*
> *To be happy forever I know*
> *Someday when spring is here*
> *We'll find our love anew*
> *And the birds will sing and wedding bells will ring*
> *Someday when my dreams come true*[5]

As Mandy Len Catron observes, "The notion that marriage is the best answer to the deep human desire for connection and belonging is incredibly seductive."[6]

We can certainly find some positive outcomes from this new, modern and romantic way of seeing marriage. Most people would prefer to have agency in choosing their life partners. And viewing women less as property and more as capable human beings who can make choices about their own lives certainly represents an improvement from previous eras of human history. However, in our day there remain several side effects and unintended consequences of the historical shift to romantic marriage.

The Soulmate Myth

In the Ancient Greek philosopher Plato's *Symposium*, one of his characters tells a story that sounds eerily like our popular conception of romantic love. Once upon a time, the storyteller tells us, people all had two heads and eight limbs. But as was often the case in the ancient world, people became the object of the wrath of the gods. As a result, Zeus split all these poor creatures in half: some became one man and one woman, some two men, and some two women. The quest of humanity becomes, according to the storyteller, to find our "other person" or our "other half."[7]

In the church culture I grew up in, this mythology went much the same, but the characters were slightly different: The idea was that God has one person that he has "willed" for you, and once you find your person, your life will be complete and fulfilled. Here we find the predictable Rom Com narrative—find your soulmate and find your bliss.[8] One counselor, exasperated with the Rom Com mythology wrote, "The fantasy is that a soulmate would never frustrate us, make us have to regulate ourselves, or create conflict."[9]

It doesn't take much reflection to recognize the absurdity of the concept of soulmate. The romantic belief that there's some "super-person" out there somewhere, and if we can just find them, they'll fulfill all our wishes and desires, sounds more like magical thinking than the thinking of a mature adult.

Nonetheless, I have met a number of single people with vision boards or long wish lists of what their elusive prince or princess will be like. Rather than working on themselves to become the kind of person who will be successful at relationships, it seems much easier to think about finding that one person for whom no work will be required at all. Astonishingly, I have met couples in counseling who were convinced they "married the wrong person" because it turns out their relationship was difficult at times and required work. A soulmate wouldn't be this much work, right?

How much the concept of soulmate diverges from "traditional" understandings of marriage can't be overstated. In pre-romantic marriages a person wanting to get married (or one's family) searched for something more like a good employee rather than a person who could meet all of one's emotional needs. I believe the concept of a "soulmate" or finding "the one" is a fool's errand. At the risk of sounding un-romantic, we create a lot of pain and suffering by perpetuating this myth.

Isolation

If a person buys into the romantic notion that their partner will be their "soulmate," it would logically follow that their partner would fulfill everything that they needed and wanted. By this reasoning, a good romantic marriage would mean that you could disengage from society and one's extended family and turn inward to find your needs met. Jewelers attempting to sell their wares still play into this cultural script: "What diamond is good enough for your best friend, lawyer, confidant, lover, girlfriend, tennis partner all rolled in to one?…What do you buy for the woman who is everyone to you?"[10] In this romantic trope, one's spouse fills countless roles to create the illusion of a crowd.

Not surprisingly, this cultural shift placed unprecedented pressure on modern marriages. Pamela Haag reflects, "The closer you are to your spouse, the less social you 'need' to be—as if the point of seeking society were to compensate for family and spousal deficiencies. Conversely, the more antisocial and emotionally reclusive the family, the stronger the love—sequestration becoming evidence not of social paucity but of romantic plenitude."[11]

Loneliness, unsurprisingly, becomes an unintended side effect of this romantic isolation. Sociologist Robert Putnam's book *Bowling Alone* paints a vivid portrait of our modern-day culture with people isolated from each other in epidemic loneliness in which those in romantic marriages "kept to themselves, asking little of their neighbors and expecting little in return."[12] Loneliness has become such a problem in the United Kingdom that in 2018, the country appointed a "Minister of Loneliness." The announcement cited the statistic that more than 9 million people "always" or "often" feel lonely in the UK.[13]

Meanwhile, in the US, former Surgeon General Vivek Murthy wrote in a Harvard Business Review article, "Loneliness is a growing health epidemic. We live in the most technologically connected age in the history of civilization, yet rates of loneliness have doubled since the 1980s. Today, over 40% of adults in America report feeling lonely, and research suggests that the real number may well be higher."[14]

Dr. Murthy's interest in loneliness research stems from public health concerns. Feeling isolated may increase one's risk of sleep disturbances, substance abuse, depression, and suicide. Additionally, a meta-analysis of studies on loneliness by Brigham Young University discovered that medical outcomes for lonely people were *worse* than other negative health risk factors, including obesity, alcoholism, and air pollution.[15]

While certainly not the only cause of the modern epidemic of loneliness, the unintended side-effects of the expectations around romantic marriage have played an important part in isolating people from extended family, friends, and communities.

Amatonormativity

Another side-effect of the invention of romantic marriage becomes what philosopher Elizabeth Brake calls "amatonormativity"—the belief that romantic love constitutes the default standard or the ideal for human beings. Amatonormativity posits that persons not in a romantic relationship have something "wrong" with them.[16] Once we say it out loud, the idea sounds absurd—especially for those who believe that an ancient Galilean rabbi embodied the ideals of what it means to be human without having a romantic partner. Obviously, there are many well-adjusted, happy people who are single—some by choice, some by circumstances.

But the way culture works in our lives, we often find internalized unexamined values finding expression. Intellectually, we may "know" amatonormativity feels absurd, but this internal attitude may prove very difficult to undo. Of course, if amatonormativity affects someone personally, they will notice it everywhere: think of songs like Dean Martin's, *You're Nobody 'Til Somebody Loves You* sung un-ironically without most people raising an eyebrow. Amatonormativity particularly paints women in a negative light, creating the trope of "crazy cat lady" or "spinster" rather than the more benign "confirmed bachelor" trope of their male counterparts.

Amatonormativity poses the danger that we will pressure people to quickly make a choice that they may not want, or one which may not be the healthiest option for them. Many people marry because of social pressure. One woman I remember telling me "I felt like the clock was ticking. If I didn't marry this guy, all the good ones would be gone. My window of opportunity to not be a social outcast was closing."

Philosopher Carrie Jenkins believes that romantic love exists in our culture to channel romance into reputable nuclear families. "Social stability—including the maintenance of privilege by the privileged—is best served by mass unawareness of the deep core of the social machinery that structures our lives and loves."[17] Consequently, challenging the notion of amatonormativity feels often like a challenge to the stabilizing effects of marriage and family.

The Madonna/Whore Complex

Romantic marriage didn't always exist. Before the modern age, women served men as bearers of children and protectors of the family line, and they had no legal standing, being under the control of their husbands. (This is still true today in some countries and cultures.) Around the beginning of the 19th century when Western culture was shifting to the age of romantic marriage, husbands still had control over their wives but men reframed the rationale for this control as "protection" of the woman.

In Victorian times, an ideal arose of women as asexual and morally pure—if a woman had sexual desires at all, it must be because she was drugged or depraved at an early age.[18] This created an odd contradiction for couples that Sigmund Freud reflected on in 1925. Freud famously wrote about the men in his day, "Where such men love they have no desire and where they desire, they cannot love."[19] In other words, Freud noticed—and also reinforced—the notion that women's humanity can be divided into two neat and tidy categories that don't overlap: they are either asexual *or* erotic, wholesome *or* polluted, nurturing *or* corrupt, respected *or* lustfully desired. This strange bifurcation came to be called the *Madonna/Whore Complex*.[20] The idea was that men desired the "whore" but wanted to marry and have children with the "madonna." This toxic side-effect of romantic marriage and what we now call "purity culture" has continued to be the source of heartache and confusion for both men and women since the advent of romantic marriage.

Cultural anthropologists tell us that language gives us the means to subtly communicate culturally significant information. When it comes to the Madonna/Whore Complex, our use of language demonstrates how this construct castigates women: Carrie Jenkins notes recent sociological research in what she calls the "slut-verses-stud phenomenon."[21] American English includes a cornucopia of negative words to describe women who stray outside of romantic norms. "Slut" is a major one. However, our language becomes weak when it comes to men who do the same, and the connotations are not as negative. "Playboy" or "Player" may be intended to be negative but sound more enjoyable than harmful. "Manwhore" or "Womanizer" may be potential counterparts, but they certainly lack "the vitriolic punch of 'slut.'"[22] Likewise, we have no English equivalent in our vernacular that glorifies and celebrates licentious women in the way that "stud" appears to glorify lustful men.

The Madonna/Whore Complex now receives a lot of resistance in the broader culture of our day,[23] but it's fully intact in Evangelical circles, which uses its familiar language and imagery:

> The evangelical cult of masculinity links patriarchal power to masculine aggression and sexual desire; its counterpoint is a submissive femininity. A man's sexual drive like his testosterone, is God-given. He is the

initiator, the piercer…Within this framework, men assign themselves the role of protector, but the protection
of women and girls is contingent on their presumed
purity and proper submission to masculine authority.[24]

It's just a short step from ideals of female purity and female submission to the corollary of toxic masculinity. Toxic
behaviors such as defending the innocence (madonna-ness)
of women are tolerated as natural expressions of masculinity
that cannot be controlled. Viewing women as property to be
defended is, of course, a cultural hangover from marriage's ori-
gins. Marriage originally evolved to control women, attesting to
paternity and ensuring the inheritance of a man's wealth by his
biological children. In its extreme expressions, protecting the
innocence of women can even be used to justify men's violent
crime through "provocation," in which men "secure lenience…
who violently killed or injured their adulterous wives and/or
the men with whom their wives were being adulterous."[25]

Sigmund Freud's psychological observations 100 years ago
about characteristics of the Madonna/Whore Complex can
still be found still alive and well today. What Freud probably
didn't realize was that he was just seeing the surface of how the
broader culture in general, and Christian culture in particular,
was also shifting in the way it understood what it meant to be
a virtuous person.

The Advent of Purity Culture

For the entirety of church history until the late 18th Century,
what it meant to be a "good person" or "virtuous" arose from
the value that a person brought to their communities: Did they

care for the poor? Did they protect the vulnerable? Did they feed the hungry? Did they look after immigrants and outsiders? These criteria were the ones that Jesus himself established to measure Christian discipleship.[26] Yet, as romantic marriage began to rise, American and European Christians began to re-frame virtue to mean something totally different. By defining virtue and Christian discipleship in purely individual terms—and as primarily the regulation of "private passions"—one could avoid caring about the needs of one's neighbors and communities—cultural obligations which were emotionally taxing, expensive, and time-consuming. Doing well for one's family became more important than adding value to society as a whole. Unfortunately, Evangelical subcultures have sometimes bought into this way of framing virtue and neglecting public goods.

The invention of purity-culture in the last two centuries quickly became a convenient way for people to ignore the important social issues of the day and instead define their goodness purely in a sexual context.[27] In one quick sleight of hand, purity culture undercut 1,800 years of church history, the teachings of Jesus, and opened the door for self-identifying Christians to self-righteously judge the vulnerable, poor, widows, immigrants, and outsiders as "devoid of virtue" (unlike themselves). Nadia Bolz-Weber observes,

> The desire to live a holy life that is pleasing to God is understandable, but this desire is also fraught with pitfalls. Our purity systems, even those established with the best intentions, do not make us holy. They only create insiders and outsiders. They are mechanisms for delivering our drug of choice: self-righteousness, as

juice from the tree of knowledge of good and evil runs down our chins.[28]

It cannot be overstated how much purity culture's insidious switch to redefine holiness merely in a sexual context avoided the harder teachings of Jesus. It became easier to look for minor breaches of decorum. Purity culture ran so deep in the cultural zeitgeist of the 19th Century Victorian age that most people refused to say the word "breast" when referring to chicken meat but instead would say "dark meat" or "white meat." This is what passed for morality.

We should note that ideas of purity have a long history. The social construct of "virginity" had arisen after the agricultural revolution long ago as an attempt to regulate purity—but it was not purity in the same sense that most people think of it in our day. "Sexual purity" in the ancient world did not describe the ethical, moral purity of a person, but the purity of *possession* that someone was giving away for a dowry. Premarital sex was thought of as a corruption of valuable property, not a violation of the person's ethical innocence. But in the reinvention of morality at the advent of purity culture, changing the meaning of the social construct we call "virginity" was an easy shift. It was now about personal virtue.

Purity culture and ideas of moral righteousness have continued to drive many young adults to marry young so that, in part, they can have guilt-free sex. Not surprisingly, wanting to have sex doesn't amount to a stable, long-term reason to get married. Additionally, the shaming around sex that drives people in conservative subcultures to marry doesn't serve as very good glue to keep them married, as the divorce rate attests.

Public Policy

If purity culture defines virtue primarily by one's sexuality, then, the logic goes, to have a virtuous society must mean to create public policy that makes sure people have sex the correct way. Much of public policy surrounding abortion, access to birth control, and sex education in public schools still has bubbling below the surface the motivations of purity culture.

In my many years inside the Evangelical world, I noticed that Evangelical culture warriors don't generally concern themselves with traditional Christian public policy issues like the homeless, the hungry, child poverty, widows, immigrants, foster children, and the poor.[29] Rather, partially by leveraging virtue primarily in sexual terms, abortion has risen to the fore as the biggest single-issue voting priority. The "vulnerable" of the Biblical text have been reimagined not as the poor, widows and orphans, but primarily as the unborn.[30] David Barnhart points out this irony eloquently:

> "The unborn" are a convenient group of people to advocate for. They never make demands of you; they are morally uncomplicated, unlike the incarcerated, addicted, or the chronically poor; they don't resent your condescension or complain that you are not politically correct; unlike widows, they don't ask you to question patriarchy; unlike orphans, they don't need money, education, or childcare; unlike aliens, they don't bring all that racial, cultural, and religious baggage that you dislike; they allow you to feel good about yourself without any work at creating or maintaining relationships; and when they are born, you can forget about them, because

they cease to be unborn. You can love the unborn and advocate for them without substantially challenging your own wealth, power, or privilege, without re-imagining social structures, apologizing, or making reparations to anyone. They are, in short, the perfect people to love if you want to claim you love Jesus, but actually dislike people who breathe. Prisoners? Immigrants? The sick? The poor? Widows? Orphans? All the groups that are specifically mentioned in the Bible? They all get thrown under the bus for the unborn.[31]

I write these words within days of the U.S. Supreme Court decision to overturn the historic Roe vs. Wade decision that guarantees abortion rights in the US. As long as I can remember, this overturning has been a goal for purity culture warriors. Yet, research shows some surprising things in which conservative Christians ought to be interested: most importantly that legal prohibition does not yield the most effective strategy to reduce the actual *number* of abortions. The Netherlands, the developed country with the lowest rate of abortions, has discovered the best way to reduce the *number* of abortions comes through commitment to sex education, teen pregnancy prevention (not abstinence education), and effective contraception.[32] Many pro-life activists fail to recognize these facts, however, because for many, the underlying motivation beneath wanting to criminalize abortion boils down not to the elimination of abortion *per se,* but can be found in a preoccupation with creating a "virtuous" society by means of control of other people's "private passions." For this same reason, they often don't want contraceptives and sex education to be widely available either—people might have pre-marital sex then. Concern with abortion and its legality arises from the logic of purity culture, not just the perceived rights of the fetus. Prior to the 1970s, Protestant Christians had little interest in or even in some cases supported abortion rights.[33]

But let's return to marriage. As the foundation of marriage in Western Civilization shifted more and more to an idea of "romantic marriage," the world began to experience its side-effects and unintended consequences. Knowing these side-effects does not just make them go away. Our internalized beliefs about romantic marriage may be unconscious, unspoken, and not easy to leave behind. Not surprisingly, marriages based on the romance model have proven to be unstable and the divorce rate in both Europe and the United States actually rose dramatically from the beginnings of romantic marriage until the 1980s. In 1891, a Cornell University professor predicted that if current marriage trends continued, by 1980 more marriages would end by divorce than by death. He was only off by 10 years.[34]

In recent years, many Evangelicals are beginning to wake up to the dangers of romantic marriage and purity culture. In the words of Kristin Kobes Du Mez, people, especially younger people, are "reassess[ing] their spiritual and sexual formation" as well as the "damage they experienced or observed within the confines of purity culture."[35] They're telling their stories and in some cases going to therapy. I believe it will take generations to undo the damage caused by the Disney Princess/Rom Com Industrial Complex I've described, including the Christian version we see in recent decades of purity culture in conservative churches. They've shaped the very way we think and perceive the world.

CHAPTER 3

The Implosion and The Possibility

"Love in action is a harsh and dreadful thing
compared with love in dreams."

–FYODOR DOSTOYEVSKY–

"The fact that an opinion has been widely held is no
evidence whatsoever that it is not utterly absurd."

–BERTRAND RUSSELL–

MENTAL SOUNDTRACK

The J. Geils Band, "Love Stinks"
Taylor Swift (feat. Bon Iver), "Exile"

I vividly remember a conversation I once had with a parishioner named Kim as she lamented the quality of her marriage. I don't remember many of the specifics of the conversation but an offhanded comment she made has always stuck with me: "I finally decided that if I'm going to be lonely, it is better to be lonely by myself." Sociological research finds this to be true: single adults have stronger social ties than married people. Being in a modern romantic marriage correlates with being more isolated from parents and siblings and being less motivated to offer emotional support or domestic help to outsiders. Romantic marriages also make people more isolated from friends and neighbors.[1] As the Russian author Anton Chekhov put it, "If you're afraid of loneliness, don't marry."[2]

Steve's perspective was typical of countless conversations I've had over the years with frustrated spouses. Over lattes at a Starbucks, Steve lamented, "I've not been happy in this marriage for years. But what am I supposed to do about it? Am I supposed to screw up my kids' lives and live in poverty so that I can roll the dice at being a little happier?" Steve's plight illustrates the truism that people don't change until the pain of not changing is greater than the pain of change. He, like many others, had not yet hit his tipping point, so was instead perpetually living with lowered expectations and low-grade melancholy.

Steve's thought process typifies people who are not completely self-absorbed: if marriage is the best environment for raising children, sticking it out for the sake of the kids must be the best thing to do, right? But current research finds that what matters for children's well-being is not the *form* the family takes but how stable the family is.[3] The stability may take the form of a two-parent family or might include extended-family structures more like those found in other cultures around the world and at most other times in human history. The volatile nature of romantic marriage makes it not a very dependable form of stability for many children. As Andrew Cherlin notes, if stability matters most for kids, then stability, not marriage, should be the primary goal.[4]

Of the roughly one-million marriages that end in divorce each year in the US, many are high-conflict and abusive—that is, they include factors like violence and addiction. However, a growing body of research indicates that most divorces happen in what researchers call "semi-happy" or "good enough" marriages.[5] The Utah Commission on Marriage concluded that 70 to 80% of divorces in their state stemmed from "soft reasons" like boredom, melancholy, and emotional fatigue.[6] And while many marriages may escape the divorce courts, they remain steadfast in the "semi-happy" camp of gloomy endurance.

Karen was a woman in my congregation that always seemed to have interested gentlemen knocking at her door and in her late twenties, she had a good job, and was smart and attractive. But much to the disappointment of her parents, she had no yearning to ever marry. She once confided in me that while she desires what most people desire—connection, intimacy, and meaningful relationships—the typical path was not for her; in her words, "I don't think being married is the best way to get what I want out of life." Nonetheless, Karen constantly felt the pressure from both her parents and cultural narratives confining her to the narrow option of romantic marriage and the nuclear family.

But Karen's intuition was accurate. Despite its supposedly universal appeal, marriage is not always satisfying. No compelling research indicates that getting married "[results] in lasting improvements in happiness, health, or any other measure of well-being."[7] Researcher Bella DePaulo observes that "When the prevailing unquestioned narrative maintains that there is only one way to live a good and happy life, too many people end up miserable."[8]

Both divorce and singlehood carry social stigma in the US, which is why many people instead prefer to remain "married and lonely," as both Steve and Kim decided to. But it makes us wonder—what if all forms of intimate relationships, like Karen's non-married life, were buttressed, celebrated, and privileged with the same vigor currently devoted to marriage?

It could be that Jesus, Paul, and the first 17 centuries of church history understood something about the dangers of marriage to our souls, things about which we are blind to today. Contemporary research demonstrates that single people like Karen connect better to the social world around them than married people. Bella DePaulo argues that being married often inadvertently makes people overlook other relationships of intimacy and support: friendships, roommates, chosen families, and wider networks of kin. Other research further reveals that single people tend to care more for their immediate families and aging parents, have more friends, and more likely engage socially with their neighbors. Single women tend to be more politically engaged than their married counterparts.[9] Interestingly, the correlation between singlehood and engagement with their communities and the world tends to be especially true for those have never married.[10] Perhaps, as Paul hinted at in the first century, the institution of marriage can actually make us worse Christians, not better ones.

In the churches I led, for years we designed programming and systems around what we understood to be the "normal" or "typical" journey of people from singlehood to marriage and parenthood.[11] We didn't realize at the time that now days only 20% of US households fit into the 1950s *Leave it to Beaver* family image of two heterosexual parents with children. Partners without children, both married and unmarried, represent 25% of US households, while millions of others live alone or un-coupled.[12] While my churches tried to prop it up, the 1950s vision of romantic marriage and family has been slowly imploding in the US. I believe it was never sustainable. In my anecdotal observations as a pastor, I have seen people dealing with the implosion of romantic marriage in several ways: sometimes it's intentional and thoughtful, sometimes reactionary and unconscious. Here are some of the responses I have seen:

Abandonment of the Institution. As giving up on marriage altogether grows in popularity in the US and Canada, this option now marks the dominant preference for Western Europeans. One Swedish professor reflecting on marriage remarked, "Traditional values are not important to us anymore. They are something we do research on—like a fossil."[13] Marriage has not delivered on the promises it's made to us, so it's easy to see why so many have become cynical about the institution.

While watching the evening news with my parents in the early 1980s, a recurring ad for Enjoli perfume stuck with me, something that seems to reflect the meaning of what it meant to be a married woman in the late 1970s and early 1980s:

'Cuz I'm a woman.
Enjoli!
I can bring home the bacon.
Enjoli!
Fry it up in a pan.
And never let you forget you're a man.

I can work till 5 o'clock.
Come home and read you tickety-tock.

Tonight I'm gonna cook for the kids.
And if it's lovin' you want, I can kiss you and give you the
shiverin' fits.[14]

As the divorce rate neared an all-time high in our country, Madison Avenue was still trying then to tell women that they could have it all: the career, the husband, the kids, and a sizzling romantic life. Some 40 years later, this whole enterprise sounds exhausting to most of us. One Third-Wave Feminist reflected, "Having it all, which sounds like a gift and a triumph, devolved into Doing It All, which sounds like a burden and a chore."[15] Conversations in the last 40 years have naturally shifted from "having it all" to conversations about "work/life balance" or simply talking about "balance."

Gritting One's Teeth. Doing marriage well can be arduous and grueling. Many people witnessed firsthand their parent's struggles and concluded this way of life was not for them. Years ago I heard a sermon in which the minister opined, "What if marriage was supposed to make you holy and not happy?" His thought stuck in my head because that's a nice way to rationalize an otherwise miserable marriage. ("I am becoming more Christ-like through all this suffering!")[16] Other marriage gurus pronounce that for marriage to work "you just have to communicate until your knuckles bleed."[17] We should just have more grit, the idea seems to be, in dealing with romantic marriage's implosion. Though the mindset that we should choose virtue over happiness traces all the way back to Aristotle, this attitude has become more and more unpopular. People are becoming unwilling to settle for lives of quiet desperation.

danielle weisberg
@danielleweisber

I love when married people are like marriage is the best!! it's hard work!!! it is work it is hard and the work is hard!! it is the hardest work I have ever worked hard at!!!! like ok I already have a job so no thank you I'm good then

12:12 AM · 12 Mar 22 · Twitter for iPhone

In a similar vein, New York Times columnist David Brooks reflects that we would be better off seeing marriage "as a social machine which, if accompanied with the right instruction manual, can be useful for achieving practical ends."[18] Marriage, for Brooks, looks a lot like rebuilding an engine in your garage—it just takes patience, a lot of elbow grease, and a few YouTube instruction videos. Stability, not fulfillment, permanence, not happiness, becomes the goal. But is it a good thing to lower marital expectations in this way, or is it just rationalizing mediocrity with a spiritual veneer? Pamela Haag prophetically warns, "In the gloaming of the romantic age, we've valorized marital mediocrity, and called it realism; we've vilified marital ambition, and called it selfish. Consequently, at a time when marriage could be anything, we very often expect it to be less."[19]

Serial Monogamy. While you aren't supposed to really plan for a marriage to fail, some people seem to be quite comfortable with understanding that romantic marriages are, by their nature, often temporary. Marriages split up so often that in many circles it's no longer surprising nor scandalous. Some have even made this expectation part of their wedding vows, replacing "'til death do us part" with something like "as long as love lasts." Perhaps there's an unspoken acknowledgement that saying "'til death do us part" meant something entirely different in an era in which the life expectancy was 35 years old, as opposed to 80 or so years today.

The idea of marriage being temporary is not new. For example, in the ancient Shia Muslim practice of *nikah mut'ah,* a couple can agree to a marriage with an expiration date to decide if they want to make their commitment permanent or not. The practice of *Nikah mut'ah* has recently been revived in our day among British Muslims.[20] In Western Europe, several thinkers and politicians have advocated for temporary marriages with an expiration date or whose status change from "temporary" to "permanent" with the arrival of children.[21] In the US, prenuptial agreements, which used to be the exclusive fare of the rich and famous, have become more and more commonplace in middle-class marriages—especially among Millennials.[22] This movement may be a gateway to re-envisioning marriage more in terms of "renting" rather than "buying."

Even if people don't go into a marriage thinking it will be temporary, romantic marriage tends to believe in the myth of the soulmate, as we discussed before. If your marriage is falling apart, the soulmate thinking goes, it's probably because your spouse tricked you into thinking they were their soulmate. How cynical, misleading and sad. I had one woman in my church who told me that she preferred online dating apps that had algorithms for matching you with others. She seemed to think that since she was so bad at choosing partners, artificial intelligence could do a much better job. It never occurred to her that the common denominator in the failed relationships was *her*. Many people inadvertently become serial monogamists with the romantic certainty that *this* time around, *this* spouse will indeed be "the one."

Scapegoating. I had a very wise divorce lawyer who in our initial consultation said to me, "I'm going to give you some free advice: some people think that the purpose of a divorce proceeding is to sit in front of a judge and have them say, 'You are right, and your partner is a scoundrel.' But that is not the purpose of the legal system. This isn't the movies. If you are looking for emotional vindication, you will be sorely disappointed in this process." We so want to blame another.

One nearly universal way people deal with the collapse of romantic marriage involves looking for a scapegoat. In Jonathon Gottschall's book, *The Story Paradox*, he recounts how the human mind naturally shapes all our experiences into a story arc. Because most good stories have a villain, people love to find a dramatic story that has a clear "hero" and "villain."[23] Divorce stories are no exception. We really want to believe that one person must be to blame for why a marriage fell apart and the other is an innocent victim. But life is not that black and white.

While I was a minister undergoing a divorce in a very conservative denomination, my Board of Ministerial Credentials desperately needed to assign blame for my marriage "failure" to someone, so they would know who to ostracize and who to defend. The criteria they used was to ask, "Who filed for divorce?" I remember being dumbfounded at this kind of naivety—as if the paperwork filer must be the rat but the receiver of the court papers was blameless. Never did it occur to them (or to be fair, to most people) that the romantic conception of marriage makes married life difficult and that even good, well-adjusted, spiritually mature people can divorce.

Doubling Down on "Traditional" Marriage. If you are familiar with the Evangelical culture, you'll know that the dominant response to the failure of romantic marriage is to say that today's marriages aren't romantic *enough.* At the same time, they invoke the idea of 'traditional" marriage. But "traditional" is a misnomer because, as chapters one and two outlined, traditional marriage was primarily about the ownership of women, inheritance rights, and survival of the family through political alliances. Consequently, one can only assume that these "traditionalist" advocates want to go back in time—but not too far back. They want to counter the worst aspects of romantic marriage model, however.

The recent so-called Marriage Movement shows a good example of this reaction to the collapse of romantic marriage. The Marriage Movement comprises a group of researchers, advocates, and "pro-marriage" forces who first combined forces at the Fourth Annual Conference of the Coalition for Family and Couples Education in Denver on June 30, 2000. Unlike the trends in Western European countries, this coalition aims to create public policy that would tip the scales in favor of heterosexual romantic marriage. According to their aims, public policy should be pro-marriage rather than marriage neutral.[24] The Marriage Movement stresses gender roles and norms from previous eras, including wifely submission. Not surprisingly, this regressive option is wildly unpopular with younger adults. When one researcher asked young women if they had to choose between remaining single or being in a traditional marriage, a crushing 80% respondents opted for singlehood.[25]

Some young adults, however, particularly those of Asian descent, have lost so much faith in romantic marriage that they are now opting for another kind of traditional marriage—arranged marriages. Aneela Rahman, an educated, 23-year-old British optometry student, had her family arrange her marriage for her. She mused, "Arranged marriages are very natural. It is something Asian people do all the time, and it is part of our culture."[26] Today, arranged marriage remains the choice for the majority of couples in India. Advocates of arranged marriages boast a marriage failure rate of 4%, but research on arranged marriages that take place in the U.S. and Europe is difficult to find.[27]

Reinventing Marriage. This last choice has some possibilities. While some are giving up or gritting their teeth, lowering expectations, looking for a scapegoat, or doubling down on traditional marriage, a few brave souls have begun questioning how we think about marriage and wondering if there might be a better way to conceptualize it. Marriage has evolved before, the thinking goes, so maybe it would be OK if it reforms again.

Marriage is not an abstraction. As Kim, Steve, and Karen and others in this chapter demonstrate, how we think about marriage affects people at the core of who they are and how they live their lives. Divorce lawyer Raoul Felder quips that "there is no product in the world (except perhaps commercial Xerox machines) that has a 50 percent breakdown rate and is still in business."[28] Romantic marriage has borne bitter fruit in our lives and our society. Change is overdue. Nadia Bolz-Weber reminds us, "[W]e should not be more loyal to an idea, a doctrine, or an interpretation of a Bible verse than we are to people. If the teachings of the church are harming the bodies and spirits of people, we should rethink those teachings."[29]

My mentor used to say that nobody likes change except babies. Indeed, change may be hard, especially when it comes to emotional topics like marriage. After Title VII passed in 1964 outlawing sex discrimination in the workforce, an airline personnel executive fretted in the Wall Street Journal, "What are we going to do when a gal walks into our office, demands a job as an airline pilot and has the credentials to qualify? Or what will we do when some guy comes in and wants to be a stewardess?"[30] Sometimes a failure of the imagination is the greatest obstacle to progress and change.

Fear of change can often cause us to catastrophize and wonder if re-thinking marriage would be a slippery slope to anarchy. Recently during lunch with a clergy colleague, I told him about this premise of this book and summarized its content. His honest gut response to me was, "So…anything goes then?" I understand that fearful impulse. I understand the anxiety that comes with re-thinking assumptions I've held most of my life and wondering where it stops. But Brian McLaren's perspective has helped me think through this "slippery slope" resistance:

[T]he slippery-slope argument—that we'd better not budge or rethink anything for fear we'll slip down into liberalism, apostasy, or some other hell—proves itself dangerous and naïve even as it tries to protect us from danger and naiveté. First, it assumes that we're already at the top of the slope, when it's just as likely that we're already at the bottom or somewhere in the middle. Second, it assumes that, even if we were at the peak, there's only one side we might be in danger of sliding down, as if the mountain had only a northern liberal slope, or an Eastern 'new age' slope without an equally dangerous Western 'old age' slope. You can back away from one danger smack over the cliff of another.[31]

The history of marriage demonstrates clearly that marriage *will* change and take on new forms. But *how* it will change will, I hope, be a better expression of what it means to love each other in the 21st century. I'm hoping to be a voice in that conversation of change. If you, dear reader, are part of a marriage, I want to offer you a theological framework from which to love more intentionally, sympathetically, and to promote the overall well-being of you and your partner.

So, what exactly are the tools that we need to re-think marriage?

CHAPTER 4

Form Follows Function

"Go outdoors and look at the trees.
The principle is the same in every one,
but see the enormous variety."

–FRANK LLOYD WRIGHT–

"In both the state and the church,
appealing to 'rules' is so often the refuge
of cowards and scoundrels."

–DIANA BUTLER BASS–

MENTAL SOUNDTRACK

Foreigner, "I Want to Know What Love Is"
Mariah Carey, "Vision of Love"

A short distance from my home in Scottsdale, Arizona lies Taliesin West, the winter home and studio of Frank Lloyd Wright from 1937 until he died 22 years later. I knew very little about Taliesin West or the architect who made it famous before I moved here. But Frank Lloyd Wright may have been the early 20th Century's "Most Interesting Man in the World." He was quirky, brilliant, arrogant, philosophical—a magnet for drama and tragedy and designer of more than 1,100 structures over a period of 70 years.

Frank Lloyd Wright uniquely integrated the shapes, forms, colors, and patterns of nature into his designs. He was known to have said, "Go outdoors and look at the trees. The principle is the same in every one, but see the enormous variety." Trees have infinite various *forms*, but their principles, their *functions,* are identical.

Wright was a disciple of the architect Louis Henry Sullivan, who may be most famous for coining the phrase, "Form follows function." In Sullivan's 1896 essay, *The Tall Office Building Artistically Considered*, he writes,

> All things in nature have a shape, that is to say, a form, an outward semblance, that tells us what they are, that distinguishes them from ourselves and from each other....It is the pervading law of all things organic and inorganic, of all things physical and metaphysical, of all things human and all things superhuman, of all true manifestations of the head, of the heart, of the soul,

that the life is recognizable in its expression, that form ever follows function.[1]

Louis Henry Sullivan and his protégé Frank Lloyd Wright were on to something important—in life, form follows function. This idea proves true not just about architecture but about the essence of life itself: the heart, the soul, and all things human.

Form also follows function in the world of ethics and morality. When a person puts *form* (actions) before *function* (love), it creates problems. Think of it this way: what if it's not a person's particular actions that are ethical in themselves, but instead, something more nuanced is at work? Maybe we need a new framework in which to conceive ethics. To borrow from the thoughts of Thomas J. Oord, "To love is act intentionally, in relational response to God and others, to promote overall well-being."[2] When we get it backwards and *function* follows *form*, we get what philosophers call "deontological ethics" (from the Greek word *deon* meaning "obligation or duty"). This school of thought puts its emphasis on obedience to moral absolutes. This means that any behavior (its *form* or expression) tends to be labeled as inherently good or evil, *regardless of the consequence.* So, for example, under this way of thought about ethics, we have a duty to do those things that are inherently good like truth telling, regardless of the outcome.

In the Christian scriptures, one can often see people responding with this mindset. If God has commanded people to not work on the Sabbath, then people act rightly if they do not work on the Sabbath. God commanded it. We don't do it. That settles it. It's simple. I don't have to use my imagination much—I just have to know what is on the "approved" list and "unapproved" list.

We first teach young children right from wrong through his way of viewing morality. We tell them what behaviors are right and what behaviors are wrong because they lack the mental ability to understand nuance. This approach sounds good in theory but for grown-ups and in practice, it can become impractical, insensitive, and simplistic. For example: do we have a moral duty to always tell the truth, even to a known murderer who asks us where their next intended victim is? What if a friend's house is burning down on the Sabbath and I am a fireman—can I put the fire out or is that breaking God's law? Is it wrong for a fire station to be staffed on the Sabbath? This approach also has another problem: you have to keep inventing rules for unforeseen situations. And the more rules you add, the more it becomes like a badly fitting, inflexible, straight jacket. In the New Testament, Jesus would often chafe against the many, many rules that had arisen in an attempt to cover every possible scenario. Let's just say Jesus is not a fan of deontological ethics.

And then there's the issue of which rule should take priority when the rules in your ethical system clash. For example: should you choose the principle of truth or the principle of love when your friend asks you if you like their new hair cut? Or, in marriage when your spouse says "Does this dress make me look fat?" Sometimes living according to deontological ethics feels like walking a tightrope!

As a pastor, I have realized that many people wanted me to give them a single right answer to every ethical question because moral ambiguity feels hard to live with. I don't doubt their sincerity and I believe these folks genuinely wanted to do the right thing. But even if they themselves couldn't work out what that "right thing" was, they liked the idea that someone, somewhere, has the one right answer. However, life's usually far more complex than that.

One of the most heartbreaking conversations I had as a pastor was with a woman named Jennifer. Jennifer had three beautiful girls but had married a complete violent loser of a man. Jennifer's husband had sexually abused her daughters but when she told her previous pastor about it, he counseled her to forgive him and stay married. Jennifer had taken to locking herself and her daughters in her room at night to protect them all from her malicious husband because her pastor had told her that if she divorced him, she would go to hell. By the time Jennifer came to me, she was desperate. The rules seemed clear to her, and she didn't want to break them and risk eternal damnation. I told Jennifer that there were greater principles at work than simple black and white rules. Because she seemed to need permission from an authority figure, I told her to divorce him, report him to the police,[3] and when she stood before God to give an account of her life, she should tell God that I told her to divorce the SOB and if God disagreed with me, I would take responsibility for her decision. She was afraid to act on her own as a moral agent who could make an intelligent, nuanced moral decision that took her and her children's own well-being into account. Jennifer's example is extreme, of course, but it clearly demonstrates how blindly following rules can lead to cruelty and absurdity. This kind of ethics appeals to the lowest common denominator of morality. It's an immature form of morality.

Jesus often railed against religious people whose deontological ethics created legalistic strait jackets dehumanizing and oppressing others. Out of frustration with some religious leaders, Jesus one time clarified, "The Sabbath was made for humankind, and not humankind for the Sabbath."[4] In other words, God has given the form (Sabbath) to human beings to be an expression of love (its intentionality). Legalistic adherence to the form (Sabbath) misses the point because *form* (the keeping of Sabbath) always follows function (the purpose is love). In Paul's writings, he similarly laments those who hold on to "the outward form of godliness but [deny] its power."[5] That's because the outward form, the command, always follows function (to act intentionally, in relational response to God and others, to promote overall well-being). In later Rabbinic teaching about work on the Sabbath, they had a similar insight: the purpose of the law is always to promote life and well-being. Thus even for orthodox Jews, it would not be breaking the Sabbath to help an animal or a person in need, but would be keeping the larger purpose of the Sabbath.

In the context of marriage, one can extrapolate from Jesus' teachings on the Sabbath to say that "Marriage was made for humankind, and not humankind for marriage." Marriage exists for the benefit of humanity, its purpose to promote the overall well-being of the partners and the other people in its sphere of influence. Another way to put this may be a bit startling—we could say that *marriage* is not sacred; *people* are sacred. More accurately, the particular form that a marriage takes is not sacred because form follows function. And what's the function? Love.

The form of what loving actions might look like shows up in as many ways as there are contexts. Although we might not use these words, every parent understands this intuitively. I have three children who are all very different. Because they are human beings, they constantly change and grow and therefore what it means to love them constantly changes. Sometimes they need comfort, sometimes reassurance, sometimes correction, sometimes a hug, sometimes an encouraging word, sometimes a swift kick in the pants, sometimes money, etc. The form of my actions may constantly change, but it always follows the function. My intent, in relational response to my children, is always to promote their overall well-being.

Notice that when Jesus taught, he did not give us an exhaustive guide to nitpicky moral decisions but rather gave us snapshots to help us see the bigger moral vision he had in mind. For example, at the end of the parable of the Good Samaritan, Jesus tells the inquiring attorney, "Go and do likewise"[6]—help your neighbor. Of course, Jesus was not expecting him to tuck that away in his head so that if he ever faced an identical situation while traveling on the road to Jericho, he would know what to do. Rather, Jesus was trying to get him—and us—to use our imaginations to see the bigger moral vision of the Kingdom of God on earth: he asks, "Who was a neighbor to the man who fell into the hands of the robbers?"[7] In this way, the lawyer to whom Jesus was speaking would be able to creatively apply to his own life the principles and habits in the story, wherever that may lead him. The function was *love of neighbor.*

Likewise, when Jesus said to the crowd, "If any want to become my followers, let them deny themselves and take up their cross daily and follow me,"[8] Jesus wasn't saying that his followers should try to follow an identical pathway to his through their lives. Rather, he was suggesting that they adopt the same habits and attitudes—like service and sacrifice—that he demonstrated on a daily basis.[9] When we do that, we will have the tools to do the right thing in any given situation. Jesus didn't give us a rulebook but instead told us stories, using short sketches or examples of the thousands of imaginative, fresh, and effective ways that we can love ourselves, our partners, our neighbors, and our world as he intended.

Most of us instinctively use this approach when we teach our kids how to live rightly. Theorists like child Psychologist Lawrence Kohlberg have observed the way children develop a moral sense.[10] When our kids are little, we give them rules like "stay away from the stove" or "don't go out in to the street." These rules signal the beginning of their moral development. Young kids don't understand the *why* and may only comply to avoid punishment, but in following the rules, it keeps them safe and happy. But we hope for them as parents that someday they will figure it out on their own and will learn to avoid situations that are painful and self-destructive. The best gift we can give our kids isn't a list of rules but the ability to make good moral decisions—to think like a grown up. Paul captures hope of maturity and the goal of loving as he writes, "When I was a child, I spoke like a child, I thought like a child, I reasoned like a child; when I became an adult, I put an end to childish ways."[11] Unfortunately, while everyone gets older, not everyone puts an end to childish ways in their ethical thinking.

Recently, the denomination I grew up in revised its official stance on human sexuality. While the statement's not surprising, it primarily focused on affirming outward forms that look a lot like a 1950s romantic marriage, rather than asking questions about how to empower people to find forms and expressions of love in their unique contemporary circumstances. Ironically, many of the people in the Bible and many Christians throughout church history wouldn't even fit into the small box that this denominational statement created.[12] The statement insisted on evaluating marriage forms without questioning how they function. For instance, in the time I spent in Africa, it became clear it was easy to project our own cultural biases and understandings of marriage forms like polygamy onto others, assuming these were mostly about sex. However, polygamy has usually functioned in these highly patriarchal cultures as an expression of love for vulnerable widows and orphans, so they could find protection and security with a male who would look after them. Context is important to understanding the morality of an action.

As a pastor, I had to work with real people and their real-world marriages. As I grew in my understanding of the way of Jesus, I began to counsel the people in my churches: when it comes to sex in the context of marriage, the form of sexual expression ethically takes a back seat to the function of love between the people. Let's look at love first. In other words, issues like how each person gender identifies, what kind of genitalia their bodies have, their kinks, and other expressions of sexuality should always appear in the context of how loving they are. Do particular actions promote acting intentionally, in relational response to God and others, to promote overall well-being? Ethical questions are not just about isolated actions.

It took me many years to realize that those who focus their ethical judgements on specific outward forms of marriage (the simple rejection of homosexuality, kinks, and so forth) without consideration of how those actions function in a relationship, practice an oversimplified and immature form of ethics that Jesus consistently railed against.[13]

I recommend a more helpful way to approach the Christian scriptures, culture, change, and the advancement of human beings: what I would call an Evolving/Fulfillment Approach. In this approach, we understand the Bible as revealing not lifeless, frozen snapshots of lives long ago and far away, but rather an evolving, dynamic story still happening. When Jesus said, "Do not think that I have come to abolish the Law or the Prophets; I have not come to abolish them but to fulfill them,"[14] he meant that he came to fulfill the law's *intention*: to extrapolate it, to bring it to life in a new context, to demonstrate its original purpose of love.

For example, when Moses brought the ten commandments down from Mount Sinai, it included this commandment: "You shall not kill."[15] That's about as basic as it gets—living with other people can be frustrating, but please try not to murder each other when you get upset. If we can all agree to use our words instead of violence to resolve conflict, it will make for a much better functioning society. That's the idea behind this prohibition.

But Jesus, during his teaching during the Sermon on The Mount, extrapolates on this commandment, brings it to life in a new context, and shows its original purpose of love: "You have heard that it was said to the people long ago, 'You shall not kill and anyone who murders will be subject to judgment.' But I tell you that anyone who is angry with a brother or sister will be subject to judgment."[16] Jesus says here, of course, don't kill each other—but the deeper issue? It's the human heart. Anger is a cancer that can cause self-destruction. That's a more nuanced ethical insight.

Later in Jesus' teaching ministry, he extrapolates on this idea even further: he brings it to life in a new context and shows its original purpose of love by telling us to "Love your neighbor as yourself."[17] So, now the idea cashes out this way: I'm going to not only give the negative prohibition of don't kill your neighbor or let your anger toward your neighbor destroy your soul, but the positive command of love your neighbor in the same way that you love yourself.

Finally, as Jesus meets with his disciples in the Upper Room, he takes it even one step further still: "Greater love has no one than this: to lay down one's life for one's friends."[18] Jesus has extrapolated all the way from "don't kill each other" to "lay down your life for each other." This Evolving/Fulfillment Approach looks something like this:

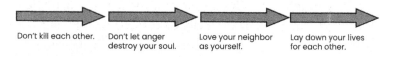

Don't kill each other.   Don't let anger destroy your soul.   Love your neighbor as yourself.   Lay down your lives for each other.

Ideas and intentions within scriptures aren't static or unchanging, but always evolving and being extrapolated, coming to life in a new context of time and place, and demonstrating the original purpose of love.

But the story hasn't stopped evolving yet. As time's gone on, we've taken this guiding principle of love Jesus taught and begun to apply it to a variety of situations—for example, in our understanding of women. In the Hebrew Bible, women appear as property to be exchanged and used. In the Gospels, Jesus treats them with respect and understanding. In the Epistles, Paul writes that in Christ there is neither slave nor free; male nor female. It has taken a while, but in 1920 we passed the 19th amendment to the constitution allowing women to vote in the United States. Maybe someday women will receive equal pay as men. These are logical extensions. The Evolving/Fulfillment Approach in this case looks something like this:

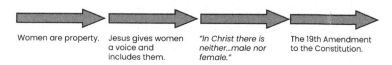

Women are property.   Jesus gives women a voice and includes them.   "In Christ there is neither...male nor female."   The 19th Amendment to the Constitution.

You can see how we have already integrated this approach in many different ethical areas: we no longer kick people out of the church for being divorced, we no longer think racism is compatible with Christian faith, we no longer think interracial marriage is sinful, and so on.

But I think slavery provides the best example of how the Evolving/Fulfillment Approach has played out. If you read through the scriptures, you will see a lot of information on how to own slaves and how slaves should be treated. Up until a couple of hundred years ago, most people thought owning slaves was morally neutral. But almost overnight that changed, and people began to view slavery as evil—and it was eventually outlawed in many countries. One person named William Wilberforce and a group of his Christian friends spearheaded a lot of the effort to change people's views, fighting the laws allowing slavery in England. There's a dirty little secret about this time in history, however: that even as Wilberforce fought for the abolition of the slave trade, he found himself condemned by many Christians in his own day. For example, when the British Parliament first defeated Wilberforce's bill for the abolition of the slave trade, the bishop of the city of Bristol (a key port in the slave trade) ordered that the church bells be rung in celebration. Wilberforce was branded a "liberal" and "unbiblical" because he had clearly abandoned the authority of scripture. And based on a straightforward reading of both the Old and New Testaments, his critics were right!

But Wilberforce believed that rather than listening to isolated proof texts which seemed to support slavery, he should look at the deeper resonance and meaning of the entirety of the scriptural story. What was it saying about the relationships between human beings? When he did this, he came up with a new understanding of slavery. Wilberforce read in Paul's letter to Philemon that he should no longer consider the runaway slave Onesimus as a slave, but Philemon should welcome him as a beloved brother.[19] Later, we can see the radical equality of all persons reinforced with Paul's words in his letter to the Galatians, "There is no longer Jew or Greek; there is no longer slave or free; there is no longer male and female, for all of you are one in Christ Jesus."[20] Again, the Evolving/Fulfillment Approach looks something like this:[21]

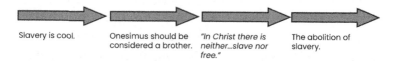

Slavery is cool.   Onesimus should be   *"In Christ there is*   The abolition of
                    considered a brother.   *neither...slave nor*   slavery.
                                             free."

So let's ask the question this book focuses on: what could marriage look like in this Evolving/Fulfillment Approach? Though still evolving and a complicated institution, I imagine we could diagram some of it to look something like this:

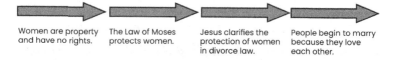

Women are property   The Law of Moses   Jesus clarifies the   People begin to marry
and have no rights.   protects women.   protection of women   because they love
                                          in divorce law.   each other.

Here's where we are now. We may not be where we need to yet, but we have come a long way. What's the next step? To re-think what might it look like to take the next step! What would it look like to leave some old unhelpful forms of marriage behind and create new forms that promote the overall well-being of our partners and others? We will turn to this next.

CHAPTER 5

I Kissed Romantic Marriage Goodbye

"When I criticize a system, they think
I criticize them and that is of course
because they fully accept the system
and identify themselves with it."

–THOMAS MERTON–

"Those who say having a childlike
faith means not asking questions
haven't met too many children."

–RACHEL HELD EVANS–

"It's supposed to be hard.
If it wasn't hard, everyone would do it.
The hard...is what makes it great."

**–TOM HANKS AS JIMMY DUGAN
IN *A LEAGUE OF THEIR OWN*–**

MENTAL SOUNDTRACK

The Beach Boys, "Wouldn't It Be Nice?"
Taylor Swift, "Blank Space"

In 1955, during the peak of romantic marriage, Frank Sinatra released the song *Love and Marriage* which said that the two "go together like a horse and carriage." Conflating love and marriage is deeply embedded in Western Civilization. After the 2015 US Supreme Court ruling decision on marriage equality for gay people, newspapers used headlines like "Love Just Won," and the hashtag #lovewins became the top-trend on Twitter. Even the language from Justice Anthony Kennedy's legal opinion seems to be right out of a Frank Sinatra song:

> No union is more profound than marriage, for it embodies the highest ideals of love, fidelity, devotion, sacrifice, and family....[M]arriage embodies a love that may endure even past death....[The] hope [of the petitioners in this case] is not to be condemned to live in loneliness, excluded from one of civilization's oldest institutions. They ask for equal dignity in the eyes of the law. The Constitution grants them that right.[1]

What's the problem with conflating love and marriage? It may not seem like a big deal at first glance and the legal opinion of the Supreme Court even sounds a little sweet and romantic, but try to see the Supreme Court's opinion through the eyes of someone who is *not* married. It implies the absence of marriage means the absence of love, painting a picture of a life doomed to loneliness and absent ideals such as devotion, sacrifice, and family. Carrie Jenkins appropriately observes, "The assumption that love and marriage are basically the same thing—or would be if you were doing life right—is damaging to the people who are in love and still unable to marry, who are in love and have no wish to marry, and who are married but receive only abuse from their spouses."[2] In spite of how romantic this sounds, love and marriage can't just be joined like a horse and carriage after all.

Frank Sinatra's song was later used, tongue placed firmly in cheek, as the theme song for the 1980s sitcom *Married with Children*. If you have seen this old Fox-TV show, it engaged in satirizing the sentimentalization of love and marriage, recorded laugh track included. We were beginning to see marriage as a social construct. What do we mean by this?

Let's first say that *all* forms of marriage, including romantic marriage, are social constructs. Saying something's a social construct doesn't mean it's not real. Think of this way: Laws are social constructs but if I drive too fast on the freeway, I will get a very real speeding ticket. Social constructs are real in that they have real consequences, but they are also dynamic and fluid. We've seen how marriage forms can vary greatly among cultures and historical eras. Why? Because we construct the rules based on our needs.

While we can certainly find a biological and evolutionary component that drives people to marry (the longing for intimacy through bonding and the drive to procreate through sexual activity, for example) we can also see how our social institutions and traditions mediate and express these biological forces. We created marriage to channel these powerful feelings into what we believe to be a safe and healthy place.

Society indoctrinates us from our earliest days how to focus these powerful emotions, usually without us being aware of it.

During recess while attending elementary school, I learned a lot about the social constructs of love and marriage without even realizing it. I memorized and recited a creed that perhaps you also recited and became part of your formation. It went like this:

_____ *and* _____ *sitting in a tree.*
K.I.S.S.I.N.G.
First comes love,
then comes marriage,
then comes a baby in a baby carriage.

This simple rhyme packs a lot of information: it tells us about what love is and how marriage functions in the world. Love involves two people (there is only room for two people in the creed), involves physical affection, and provides the means for reproduction and the formation of a nuclear family. Of course, as I grew up, I received a bounty of other cultural messages about love and marriage in music, art, literature, Romantic Comedies, television commercials, and magazines. These imparted to me how love, marriage, sex, and reproduction should work—and not work. In the words of the TV character Kilgrave in *Jessica Jones*, "I am new to love, but I do know what it looks like. I do watch television!"[3]

With all these social constructs firmly in place in my mind and heart, I began my career as a pastor in what may be the easiest and one of the most enjoyable jobs in human history: youth ministry. Before cell phones and the internet, it wasn't difficult to impress or entertain adolescents for hours in suburban Idaho with games like "Winkum" and "Chubby Bunny."[4] But the deep anxiety of a lot of baby boomer parents in the late

1980s centered on how to keep their teenagers from having sex. So, drawing on resources from Evangelical celebrities like Josh McDowell, I became pretty good at extolling the virtues of abstinence to wide-eyed adolescents, telling them about love and marriage although I was unmarried myself.

Among Evangelicals, the purity movement would find its apex in 1997 when a 19-year-old, home-schooled Evangelical young man named Josh Harris wrote a critique of romantic marriage called *I Kissed Dating Goodbye*.[5] The book sold over 1.2 million copies and, in many ways, single-handedly changed the conversation about dating and marriage in Evangelical circles. Harris critiqued the way in which marriage had evolved to be romantic-based and rooted in personal choice, arguing this was inherently destructive to long-term happiness in marriages.

In some ways, Josh Harris was right. Romantic marriage in its current form is unsustainable. What Mr. Harris got wrong was this: instead of looking to the future, he looked to the past, offering a model of dating and marriage that was *more* patriarchal and *more* immersed in purity culture than ever.[6] But we have to ask: what if our critique of romantic marriage looked instead to the future and reflected the social and cultural changes that humanity has experienced instead of trying to fit what God is doing in our age into the "old wineskins" of the past?[7]

Inside a fake living room on the campus of Northwestern University in Evanston, Illinois, a researcher and professor named Eli Finkel does ground-breaking research on modern marriage in the United States. Dr. Finkel confesses, "My wife finds it hilarious that I'm a marriage expert!" But new and interesting discussions are coming out of his research into how marriage forms have changed in recent years.

In his book, *The All-or-Nothing Marriage*, Dr. Finkel observes that marriage over the years has evolved to parallel Abraham Maslow's famous framework in his 1943 paper, *A Theory of Human Motivation*.[8] Many people are familiar with Maslow's Pyramid of Human Needs. Maslow proposed that all human beings have needs. He said these needs can be arranged in a hierarchy with some being more central, primitive, or basic than others. He believed once more basic needs are met (oxygen, hunger, thirst, shelter), human beings become more interested in other, "higher" needs (such as belonging, love, esteem, and so forth). Maslow's "hierarchy" of needs often diagrams something like this:

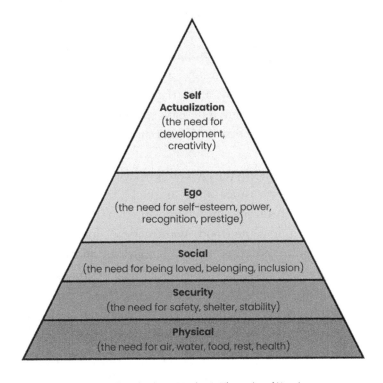

FIGURE 3 – Abraham Maslow's Hierarchy of Needs

Eli Finkel noticed that marriage's original function was to help enable human beings to physically survive. Once human beings had adequate caloric intake and a roof over their heads, they began to evolve new forms of marriages that reflected new functions higher on the pyramid. People began to look a little higher on the pyramid to marriage for security: this included economic safety, control, predictability, and physical safety. Then beginning in the late 18th Century, marriage began, for the first time, to ask even higher "social" questions about belonging, love, and inclusion. This was the beginning of romantic marriage.

According to Eli Finkel, marriages in our day now not only are supposed to provide love, cooperation, and a sense of belonging to a family and community, we expect even higher level needs to be met such as prestige, autonomy, personal growth, and self-expression. Today, a marriage seemingly functions to help the individuals within it develop self-esteem, express themselves, and become the best versions of themselves. Finkel writes,

[D]iverse forces [have] increasingly freighted marriage in America over time, piling so much expectation and responsibility on this one relationship that it threatened to buckle under the strain. We Americans increasingly look to our spouse to be our best friend and closest confidant, to provide sizzling sex, to help us grow as individuals—the list goes on. At the same time, we spend less time with our friends, parents, and siblings, and we are less engaged in organized civic activities outside the home. Collectively, these forces place tremendous pressure on the marital bond, and few marriages are able to withstand the stress.[9]

We see the cultural zeitgeist of high-altitude relationships reflected in popular romantic comedies. Tom Cruise's character, Jerry, declares his love to Renee Zellweger's character, Dorothy, in *Jerry McGuire* declaring, "You complete me," and Jack Nicholson's character, Melvin, says to Helen Hunt's character, Carol, in the movie *As Good as It Gets*, "You make me want to be a better man." Most people now seek marriage or long-term relationships with their partners in the service of self-actualization. Pamela Drukerman observes:

> Women of my grandmother's generation didn't usually fret about whether their marriages were personally fulfilling or not. But since it became much easier to divorce in the 1960s, we've been holding our marriages—and our lives—to an extremely high standard. We strive for perfect health and fitness, and we expect emotionally satisfying marriages and complete fidelity.[10]

In his research, Dr. Finkel re-conceptualized Maslow's Hierarchy of Needs in the context of marriage not as a simple triangle but as a mountain—what he called "Mount Maslow."

He posits that the higher a marriage "climbs" on the mountain, the thinner the air. Lower altitude needs do not require nearly as much "oxygen" (time and energy) as higher altitude needs. As marriages have become increasingly focused on higher and higher altitudes, they require more and more "oxygenation" or greater investment in each other's emotional and psychological needs. According to Finkel, expecting higher altitude results without this oxygenation sets us up with a prescription for "suffocation—or lethargy, conflict, and perhaps divorce."[11]

Category of Need	Specific Examples	Mount Maslow
Self-Actualization	• Self-expression • Personal growth • Autonomy • Spontaneity • Veridical self-assessment	
Esteem	• Self-esteem • Self-respect • Sense of mastery • Prestige • Respect from others	
Belonging and Love	• Love for others • Being loved by others • Trust in others • Sexual intimacy • Belonging to a group	
Safety	• Economic security • Control • Predictability • Psychological safety • Physical safety	
Physiological	• Hunger • Thirst • Warmth • Sleep • Respiration	

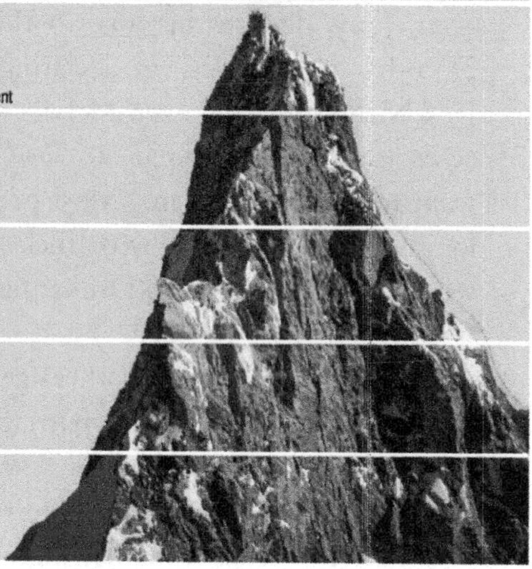

FIGURE 4 – Mount Maslow (Eli Finkel, The All or Nothing Marriage, 24).

Add the reality of a longer life expectancy, and today, much more than in previous generations, the weight of this "freighting" compounds over time. At the end of the 19th Century, two-thirds of American marriages ended with the death of one partner within 40 years.[12] In 1976, as life expectancies increased, so did divorce rates. Just 76 years later, American marriages that ended by death had dropped to around only one third.[13]

Elizabeth's Gilbert's memoir *Eat. Pray. Love.* shows a clear picture of a contemporary marriage that climbed Mount Maslow and suffocated for lack of oxygen. Hers was a marriage in which the partners had all the physiological, safety, and belonging and love needs firmly intact. Yet Gilbert reflects in her memoir:

I will…not discuss here all the reasons why I *did* still want to be his wife, or all his wonderfulness, or why I loved him and why I had married him and why I was unable to imagine life without him. I won't open any of that. Let it be sufficient to that, on this night, he was still my lighthouse and my albatross in equal measure. The only thing more unthinkable than leaving was staying; the only thing more impossible than staying was leaving. I didn't want to destroy anything or anybody. I just wanted to slip quietly out the back door, without causing any fuss or consequences, and then not stop running until I reached Greenland.[14]

Our shifting of marriage expectations toward "higher altitude" needs conceals a double-edge sword. On one hand, when a marriage works, focusing on higher-altitude needs correlates with martial quality and personal well-being. Contemporary research affirms this observation. Sociologists Bruce Headey, Ruut Veenhoven, and Alex Wearing have discovered that when a high-altitude marriage is going well, it can be the single most robust predictor of one's global life happiness.[15] As Maslow himself observed many years ago, "Higher need gratifications produce more desirable subjective results, i.e., more profound happiness, serenity, and richness of the inner life."[16] In other words, when high-altitude marriages work, they work really well. Perhaps at no time in human history has marriage had the potential to be as fulfilling as it is today.

On the other hand, for a variety of social and cultural reasons the amount of time, energy, and resources available to couples to invest in their marriages has decreased over time. This makes higher altitude needs more and more difficult to fulfill. Finkel writes, "In a cruel cultural twist, just as we have increasingly looked to our marriage to help us fulfill higher-level needs, we have decreasingly invested the time and energy required for the marriage to meet these expectations."[17] So while the potential for fulfillment remains greater than ever, it remains elusive for the vast majority of us. The research cited earlier in this book is reflective of this truth: for most people marriage does not make us happy. Taylor Swift poetically captures this paradox well:

> *Because we're young, and we're reckless,*
> *we'll take this way too far*
> *It'll leave you breathless,*
> *Or with a nasty scar.*[18]

Eli Finkel uses a poignant monologue by Miles, a character played by Paul Giamatti in the movie *Sideways,* to illustrate how to think of this paradox in relationships. Miles, discussing the wine grape Pinot Noir, waxes eloquent:

It's a hard grape to grow…It's thin-skinned, temperamental, ripens early. It's not a survivor like Cabernet, which can just grow anywhere and thrive even when neglected. No, Pinot needs constant care and attention. In fact, it can only grow in these really specific little tucked-away corners of the world. And only the most patient and nurturing of growers can do it, really. Only somebody who really takes the time to understand Pinot's potential can then coax it into its fullest expression. Then, I mean, its flavors, they're just the most haunting and brilliant and thrilling and subtle and ancient on the planet.[19]

In short, Finkel makes the analogy that surviving in the lower stratospheres of marriage proves not nearly as complicated, like Cabernet ("[it] can grow anywhere and thrive even when neglected"). But for contemporary marriages to thrive in higher altitudes, they need to double down on the time and energy invested to meet the marriage's increasing demands—they are more like Pinot Noir ("[it] needs constant care and attention"). These rare marriages can become, however, "the most haunting and brilliant and thrilling and subtle and ancient on the planet."

This analogy could either be really encouraging, challenging, or completely deflating, depending on one's life situation. Some will hear these words and idealistically decide they will be the few, the proud, and aim for the high-altitude ("Pinot Noir") marriage. Armed with all the oxygen they need, they will boldly climb Mount Maslow together hand-in-hand.

But unfortunately, many others will hear these words and think of the unfolded laundry, the car that needs an oil change, the kids who need to get to soccer practice, the food that needs to be prepared, or their overdue work assignments and feel as if they have been handed yet another "should" to add to their "to do" list. Or what if they have a partner who would rather contentedly sit by the pool with their face buried in their iPhone rather than climb some dumb mountain? It takes two to climb Mount Maslow, after all.

Researchers like Eli Finkel have written well-researched books that serve as an invaluable resource to those interested in growing a delicate Pinot Noir relationship. A more interesting—and practical—question to me: what might marriage look like for most people who are *not* independently wealthy; don't work only 20 hours a week; don't have perfect physical health; haven't worked through all the psychological issues of their past—AND perhaps don't have a partner who wants to climb with them? What about them?

While Eli Finkel has called his book, *The All or Nothing Marriage*, I think there's perhaps a third option as well. What if all the needs on Mount Maslow weren't met by our romantic partners? What if we diversified the ways and forms through which these needs were met? It may be that going back to some past models of marriage could hold the key to how marriage could work for us in the future.

CHAPTER 6

Clear is Kind. Unclear is Unkind.

"Happiness equals expectation minus reality."

—RAY MAGLIOZZI FROM NPR'S *CAR TALK*—

"In desperate love, we always invent the characters
of our partners, demanding they be what we need of
them, and then feeling devastated when they refuse
to perform the role we created in the first place."

—ELIZABETH GILBERT, *EAT, PRAY, LOVE*—

"Love is an ideal thing, marriage a real thing;
a confusion of the real with the ideal
never goes unpunished."

—JOHANN WOLFGANG VON GOETHE—

MENTAL SOUNDTRACK

Adele, "Rolling in The Deep (We Could Have Had It All)"
Coldplay (feat. The Chainsmokers), "Something Just
Like This"

Several years ago I had a conversation with a parishioner named Becky who was single and looking to find a partner. She was a goal oriented, successful person and thought of leveraging her professional skills for dating life success. She had created an Excel spreadsheet to list all the "must haves," "nice to haves," and "deal breakers" for any potential new partners. As she met various gentlemen, she would enter them into her spreadsheet and see how they measured up to her goals and expectations, coming up with a composite score. We teased Becky a lot about her approach, yet years later, a couple of things about Becky's tactic have stuck with me.

First, few people explicitly list their expectations in a partner. Often our expectations derive from unconscious beliefs inherited from our families of origin, our religious upbringing, our past experiences, and cultural expectations from Romantic Comedies. Sometimes people remain unaware of their expectations until they find themselves disappointed. It's rare to both be aware of your expectations and be good at communicating those expectations to a partner.

Second, since Becky was so successful in her professional life, you can imagine the level of expectation she had for her potential partner. We used to tease Becky that a billionaire with the character of Jesus and the looks of Channing Tatum still wouldn't meet her expectations! While I certainly understand Becky's impulse and don't think people should settle for mediocrity in relationships, I now wonder about the wisdom of trying to win the lottery with one super-person. What if instead

Becky thought about marriage relationships more like our ancestors did, recognizing that one person rarely meets all our
needs? The Mount Maslow hierarchy of needs can very rarely
be climbed with one single, other person—and even if we win
the relational lottery and find "the one," this puts us in a risky
situation. What happens if the other person gets hit by a bus
and dies? Or falls in love with a co-worker?

Divorce crushes people in no small part because they depend on their partners arduously to climb up Mount Maslow
with them, relying on them for not just physiological needs
and safety needs, but also belonging needs, love needs, esteem
needs, and self-actualization needs. One philosopher of love
reflected:

> The real fault in the [marital conflict] situation lies in
> the ethos of modern marriage, with its insane ambitions
> and its insistence that one person can plausibly hope to
> embody the eternal sexual and emotional solution to
> another's every need. Taking a step back, what distin-
> guishes modern marriage from its historical precedents
> is its fundamental tenet that all our desires for love, sex
> and family ought to reside in the selfsame person. No
> other society has been so stringent or so hopeful about
> the institution of marriage, nor ultimately, as a conse-
> quence, so disappointed in it.[1]

When counselors (and others in helping professions) go
through training, they learn the dangers of "dual" relationships
or "dual" roles, and the need to avoid them. The practice of dual
relationships avoidance recognizes it's difficult, if not impossible, to both be someone's counselor as well as their friend, or

co-worker, or bowling partner (or have any other role in their lives.) As a pastor, I regularly found that if a person confessed their deepest, darkest secrets to me in a counseling context, it wouldn't take long until they found another church to attend. I imagine that showing up on a Sunday and having to interact socially with me reminded them of all the things in their heart and soul that they didn't want to face or have others to know.

Dual relationships can sometimes be tricky in family relationships as well. Sometimes our kids won't listen to the advice we give them but when another adult offers the very same advice in passing, our child might think it's brilliant. Similarly, anyone who has coached youth sports knows how hard it can be to coach your own kid. Or teach your own kid.

This suggests that our intimate partners generally don't make very good life coaches or accountability partners. We instinctively want them to play the role of emotional supporter, not the heavy in our lives. A partner probably can't do both. It's just a fact: the diversity of roles that we need to climb Mount Maslow may simply be impossible to find in one person.

We all need relational diversity. I'm reminded of an interview I read with the cartoonist Scott Adams, where he reflected on what advice he would give to his 30-year-old self. Adams explained that since he was a teenager, he had had many stress-related medical problems. As a result, he has spent much of his adult life trying to find ways to avoid stress:

> I would consider myself a world champion at avoiding stress at this point in dozens of different ways. A lot of it is just how you look at the world, but most of it really is the process of diversification. I'm not going to worry about losing one friend if I have a hundred, [but] if I

have two friends, I'm really going to be worried. I'm not going to worry about losing my job because my one boss is going to fire me, because I have thousands of bosses at newspapers everywhere...I don't worry about my stock picks because I have a diverse portfolio. Diversification works in almost every area of your life to reduce your stress.[2]

I would suggest that we can think wisely and prudently about marriage by looking at the way people have viewed it through most of human history: stressing diversification and not weighing down a marriage with the expectation that one super-person will be all things to another person.

Because we have such high expectations for marriage in our day, it's crucial to develop a skill set for understanding and communicating our expectations for each unique marriage. Every marriage brings together two personalities and their histories; their emotional wounds, triggers, and families of origin; their hopes, dreams, and love languages; their physical characteristics, strengths, weaknesses, insecurities, and other unique data points. Understanding all this consciously allows us to be more gracious to ourselves and others when a marriage doesn't follow the expectations or norms of the crowd. When marriages "work," they work not because they conform to some abstract ideal, but because they accommodate the uniqueness of the participants. Let's face it: ideas of what is "normal" can pathologize diversity.

In his book, *The End of Average*, educator Todd Rose observes, "From the cradle to the grave, you are measured against the ever-present yardstick of the average, judged according to how closely you approximate it or how far you are able to exceed it."[3] Schools, workplaces, and institutions like marriage end up creating forms for the "average" person to aspire to and expects everyone to fit neatly into that form. But Rose notes that there's no such thing as an "average" person and no such thing as an "average" marriage. The concept of "average" doesn't help us thrive at all—in fact, it's fundamentally flawed.

In a church I served, I knew a couple named Al and Betty who had been married for over 60 years. By this time in their lives, their health was failing, and they had reached the twilight of their time on Earth. I was struck by how much their marriage had changed over the years. The once starry-eyed newlyweds had long ago settled into a comfortable routine. Al and Betty had weathered all kinds of crises in their years together—financial crises, health crises, the sudden death of a sibling, as well as the many changes that time, children, and technology bring us all. Throughout these many changes, they had redefined and re-committed themselves to the ever-new realities of their lives together. They showed me how fluid good marriages need to be—long-term marital health involves surviving the unique, shifting circumstances of life over time.

As I write this chapter, I'm in the middle of selling my home and purchasing and remodeling another one. With cordless drill in hand, I realize how much relationships can be like houses. For some people, their houses function like their relationships: they're simple, and they're just about survival—basically a roof over their heads and a safe place to sleep at night. For others, their homes express themselves, not only in their design and floor plan, but also in decoration. As I work on my new home, I see how it often takes a lot of work to shape a house into a home that expresses ourselves.

There may be other times in our lives when we have to re-invent the whole house. Maybe we have a child, or an aging parent moves in, or now we are working remotely—and we need to adjust and reimagine everything to accommodate that new reality. Sometimes we decide that the house might be damaged beyond repair ("condemned") and no longer habitable. Or we may ask ourselves the difficult question, "Is it possible to remodel this house, or has it outlived its usefulness for the season for which we needed it, and we now need to move on?"

Rarely do we have the luxury of sitting back and saying, "Whew. This house functions exactly the way I want it." Both our homes and life circumstances are constantly in flux. As Al and Betty demonstrated, we constantly evolve in learning what it means to love a partner. We must think about *what* needs on Mount Maslow we're expecting from a partner and *how* those needs can be communicated and met—and re-communicated over time. I happen to like the current trend speaking of "love languages" as a good way to frame this conversation. Gary Chapman made a good start by naming five love languages,[4] but I have some friends who love to joke about their love languages being things like "sarcasm," "laundry folding," and "collaborative Netflix binge-watching"—we really can see an infinity of languages of love. To Chapman's credit, though, it's always a good start to ask, "What is the best way to love this person in a way in which *they* understand?"

As a pastor using psychological tools I have instinctively wondered, "What does it look like for marriage to evolve in a practical sense? How do these ideas and commitments translate to the real world?" As I've thought more about Eli Finkel's "Mount Maslow" of human needs, I've played around with Dr. Finkel's descriptions and tried to make them less abstract. At one point I correlated some contemporary aspects of marriage with Maslow's Hierarchy myself and re-worked his diagram to look something like this:

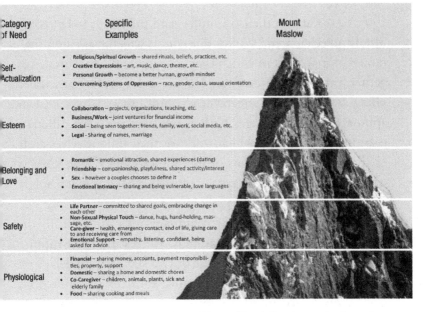

Category of Need	Specific Examples	Mount Maslow
Self-Actualization	• **Religious/Spiritual Growth** – shared rituals, beliefs, practices, etc. • **Creative Expressions** – art, music, dance, theater, etc. • **Personal Growth** – become a better human, growth mindset • **Overcoming Systems of Oppression** – race, gender, class, sexual orientation	
Esteem	• **Collaboration** – projects, organizations, teaching, etc. • **Business/Work** – joint ventures for financial income • **Social** – being seen together: friends, family, work, social media, etc. • **Legal** - Sharing of names, marriage	
Belonging and Love	• **Romantic** – emotional attraction, shared experiences (dating) • **Friendship** – companionship, playfulness, shared activity/interest • **Sex** - however a couples chooses to define it • **Emotional Intimacy** – sharing and being vulnerable, love languages	
Safety	• **Life Partner** – committed to shared goals, embracing change in each other • **Non-Sexual Physical Touch** – dance, hugs, hand-holding, massage, etc. • **Care-giver** - health, emergency contact, end of life, giving care to and receiving care from • **Emotional Support** – empathy, listening, confidant, being asked for advice	
Physiological	• **Financial** – sharing money, accounts, payment responsibilities, property, support • **Domestic** – sharing a home and domestic chores • **Co-Caregiver** – children, animals, plants, sick and elderly family • **Food** – sharing cooking and meals	

FIGURE 5 – Eli Finkel's "Mount Maslow" with specific relational aspects of marriage overlaid.

Eli Finkel observes, as we saw, that many current couples raise their expectations for marriage higher and higher up Mount Maslow. I've noticed anecdotally an increasing trend in recent years in which some couples have begun to shed traditional forms of marriage and re-define marriage in a way that works for them. One couple I know has decided they don't want to have children.[5] Another keeps separate finances including separate checking accounts. Another couple lives their lives apart most of the time, but then they come together for romantic liaisons. One woman I know finds her emotional needs met in other people more emotionally available to her than her partner. Another couple has a renewable marriage agreement they re-visit every seven years; they perceive that some marriages don't necessarily "fail" so much as they die and may just come to the end of their triumph—and this needs to be recognized and celebrated.[6] I know one couple who has a "parenting" model of marriage, in which they co-parent and cohabitate together but otherwise don't depend on each other for any other safety, belonging, or esteem needs. Still others I have known approach their marriages with forms that are very different than most others, but which work for their unique selves and/or their distinctive seasons of life. Philosopher Carrie Jenkins concludes, "I have yet to see convincing evidence that a single standard model for human relationships is hardwired into our biology…As a species, modern humans are a romantically diverse bunch. What 'comes naturally' to us varies: our infinite variety cannot be reduced to one or two standard models."[7]

As discussed in Chapter 4, since form follows function, what these varied marriages look like or what they do (their forms or expression) may not be as important as how they function in the participant's life. Rather than ask what a marriage *is* (focusing on the form) we can ask a better question: are the partners acting intentionally, in relational response to God and others, to promote overall well-being?

When we don't allow the form a marriage takes some flexibility, it can become a straitjacket that forces people into difficult situations. For example, a friend of mine's father and mother were married for 40 years when her father's mental function deteriorated with the dementia of Alzheimer's. They were fortunate to find a great care facility for him that lovingly cared for him and all his needs. However, he was no longer able to recognize his spouse and children and for all practical and emotional purposes, their marriage was over. After about five years of being alone, my friend's mother met a man and wanted to begin a relationship with him, but her Evangelical background kept her from divorcing her husband, even in a "compassionate" divorce. So, while her husband wound down his final couple of years, they moved in together and her new partner and her would jointly visit her husband at the nursing home together. She was the subject of gossip in their church community but after her husband died, she felt she finally had the freedom to marry her new partner.

Honestly, it takes a lot of courage to break free from cultural expectations and norms. But if the form of your love for another person does not always conform to the normative standards of your community and causes tribal shaming, just know that you are in good company with most of the people of the Hebrew Scriptures and most of human history. Most of them would not fit in to some people's narrow definitions of marriage.

Many individuals would rather comfortably settle with existing cultural norms than to re-think or re-define their relational expectations. In her thoughtful cultural observation of marriage, Pamela Haag notices, "Even though we have both the means (the freedom) and the incentive (the melancholy) to bring about change, we don't really use that freedom to figure out how marriage might evolve—substantively, not superficially—into something better and more satisfying."[8]

Andie Nordren's concept of "Relationship Anarchy" contains some nuggets of insight helpful in framing relational expectations on the Maslow Mountain. In broad and over-simplified terms, Relationship Anarchy takes its cue from political anarchy, arguing that relationships should not be bound by expectations not agreed upon by both parties.[9] The idea is that partners should openly communicate those expectations upfront and not assume that cultural beliefs should drive the expectations in their relationship.

Relational Anarchy thrives on consent and communication. It starts with attraction and affection between two people and then add-ons can include sex, kids, home building, family building, owning a dog together, and so on. Relationship Anarchists will often use a "menu" to pick from a smorgasbord or buffet of relational options for themselves and their partners. They then re-visit this menu, like a trip to the all-you-can-eat buffet, on a regular basis as the relationship and/or environment changes, in order to clarify the expectations of their relationship. This model of marriage recognizes there's really no "standard model" when it comes to human relationships; all relationships are unique and constantly evolving.

Below, I've provided a sample Relational Anarchy menu using the relational aspects of marriage in the previous figure of Mount Maslow:[10]

Relationship Menu

To form a relationship, pick any number of "items" from the menu below. Both people must agree in order for it to be part of the relationship. Review the list regularly as circumstances or the relationship changes to avoid conflict or disappointment.

■ MUST HAVE   ☺ LIKE TO HAVE   [?] MAYBE   ⊘ NOT IN THIS RELATIONSHIP

Physiological Needs

Financial	Domestic	Food	Co-Caregiver
☐ Shared bank accounts	☐ Having a key	☐ Collaborative cooking/ cleaning	☐ Pregnancy/children to-gether/co-parenting
☐ Shared payments of bills	☐ Cohabitation	☐ Collaborative menu selec-tion	☐ Sharing Pet(s)
☐ Shared property and/or real estate	☐ Home ownership	☐ Regular meals together	☐ Caring for sick and/or elderly family members
☐ Mutual contributions to vacations/activity fund	☐ Shared domestic respon-sibilities	☐ _____	☐ _____
☐ Financial support	☐ _____	☐ _____	☐ _____
☐ Large gifts	☐ _____		
☐ Complete financial inte-gration			
☐ _____			
☐ _____			

Safety Needs

Emotional Support	Care-Giver	Non-Sexual Touch	Life Partner
☐ Empathetic listening	☐ Emergency contact per-son	☐ Dance	☐ Planning for the future
☐ Being a safe place to be vulnerable	☐ Support through physical health challenges	☐ Hugs	☐ Expectation of long-term involvement
☐ Keeping secrets	☐ Support through mental health challenges	☐ Hand holding	☐ Commitment to working through challenges
☐ Giving advice	☐ Hospice/end of life care	☐ Massage	☐ Commitment to relation-ship maintenance
☐ _____	☐ _____	☐ _____	☐ _____
☐ _____	☐ _____	☐ _____	☐ _____

Belonging and Love Needs

Emotional Intimacy	Sex	Friendship	Romantic
☐ Sharing vulnerable feelings ☐ Saying "I love you" ☐ Sharing stories about the past ☐ Sharing hopes for the future ☐ _____ ☐ _____	☐ PDA ☐ Kissing ☐ Sex ☐ _____ ☐ _____	☐ Expressing happiness and joy ☐ Knowing personal likes/dislikes (ie- favorite foods) ☐ Texting/Frequent check-ins ☐ _____ ☐ _____	☐ Using terms of endearment ☐ Joint vacations ☐ Regularly scheduled time together/date nights ☐ Speaking each other's love languages ☐ _____

Esteem Needs

Legal	Social	Business/Work	Collaboration
☐ Being recognized by the state as legally married ☐ Having relationship labels ("husband"/ "wife", etc.) ☐ Wills/trusts/power of attorney ☐ Living will/ medical power of attorney ☐ _____	☐ Presenting as a couple in public settings ☐ Meeting children ☐ Meeting family of origin ☐ Involvement with friend group ☐ "Facebook Official" ☐ Being +1 for social events ☐ _____	☐ Meeting co-workers ☐ Co-owning a business ☐ Being co-workers ☐ _____ ☐ _____	☐ Partnering with projects ☐ Volunteering together at nonprofits ☐ Shared Google calendar/ calendar management ☐ Co-teaching ☐ _____ ☐ _____

Self-Actualization Needs

Overcoming Systems of Oppression	Personal Growth	Creative Expression	Spiritual Growth
☐ Equal distribution of relationship power ☐ Shared political beliefs/ political involvement ☐ _____ ☐ _____	☐ Balance of time together and apart ☐ Support to pursue independent interests ☐ _____ ☐ _____	☐ Shared artistic expression (ie - music, painting, etc.) ☐ Dance ☐ Co-writing ☐ _____ ☐ _____	☐ Shared religious rituals (ie – church attendance) ☐ Shared religious beliefs ☐ Shared religious spiritual practices (ie- prayer, fasting, learning, worship) ☐ _____

Alcoholics Anonymous, as part of their program of recovery, repeats a truism that says, "Clear is kind; unclear is unkind." In recent years, researcher Brené Brown has adopted this saying to describe how healthy relationships function.[11] She notes that communicating half-truths in order to make someone else (or ourselves) feel better is unkind. And it's unkind to not be able to communicate hopes, dreams, expectations, or fears to a marriage partner because it feels too difficult—especially if we hold the other partner accountable or blame them for not meeting our unspoken needs.

In contrast, while it's not easy, it's an expression of kindness to have the hard conversation about needs and expectations. Brené Brown calls these conversations "a rumble."

> For us, this is more than just a weird West Side Story way to say, "Let's have a real conversation, even if it's tough." It's become a serious intention and a behavioral cue or reminder. A rumble is a discussion, conversation, or meeting defined by a commitment to lean into vulnerability, to stay curious and generous, to stick with the messy middle of problem identification and solving, to take a break and circle back when necessary, to be fearless in owning our parts, and, as psychologist Harriet Lerner teaches, to listen with the same passion with which we want to be heard.[12]

Deciding there are aspects of Maslow's Mountain for which it's better to rely on someone else other than the marriage partner can feel like one is saying, "you are inadequate." But every one of us inadequately meets our partner's needs—we simply can't to be all things to our significant others. None of us are superman or superwoman. Some of these conversations surrounding different aspects of one's relationship will be relatively easy and obvious for partners: the logistics of food, communication methods, what titles to call each other, emotional intimacy, and so on. Other aspects can easily be fraught with landmines: parenting styles, in-laws, and finances, and sex, for example.

Up until this point, I've given very little direct attention to the one aspect of the "Belonging and Love" needs on Mount Maslow that for most people will be the greatest struggle. But this struggle is truly the elephant in the room—especially in Evangelical circles. As such I need to address the ethics of it specifically and directly. So let's talk about sex.

CHAPTER 7

Neither Animals nor Angels

"In London alone, there are 80,000 prostitutes. What are they but...human sacrifices offered up on the altar of monogamy?"

−ARTHUR SCHOPENHAUER−

"I did not have sexual relations with that woman."

−PRESIDENT WILLIAM JEFFERSON CLINTON−

"Sometimes the questions are complicated and the answers are simple."

−DR. SEUSS−

MENTAL SOUNDTRACK

Alanis Morrissette, "You Oughta Know"
Taylor Swift, "Betty"

I once did an informal survey of some of my friends and asked them, "how did you first hear about sex?" Only one of them told me that they first heard about sex from one of their parents. Most of them learned about sex through other kids or pornography. Some of the stories they told were funny, others tragic. I have one friend who told me that the only time his parents ever talked to him about sex was the day he left for college. His mother took him aside and said, "I want you to be careful. There are bad girls at college." (My friend confessed that he thought to himself, "Really? Where?")

If you grew up in a conservative religious environment like I did, you know that sexuality was rarely talked about or seldom cast in a positive light. Country music artist Butch Hancock sums it up well: "Life in Lubbock, Texas taught me two things: One is that God loves you and you're going to burn in hell. The other is that sex is the most awful, filthy thing on earth, and you should save it for someone you love."

Many of us have were fed a lot of harmful and inaccurate ideas about sex. As a result, countless numbers of us have wounds when it comes to sex and sexuality, secret shame, unresolved guilt, or unresolved resentment over something that has happened to us. And research shows shame and difficulty around sexuality is getting worse, not better.[1] Our children and grandchildren are inheriting a heavy load.

Neither Animals nor Angels[2]

Some people tend to view human sexuality in very primal terms. The thought process goes like this: underneath all our "civilized" exterior, we are at our essence, animals. Animals have sex because it's in their DNA and their chemical makeup drives them to it. Therefore, we might as well lose ourselves in whatever cravings or desires we might have because, as the saying goes, "what happens in Vegas, stays in Vegas."

It can be helpful to think of human beings as animals. Modern medicine gives us longer life expectancies and a higher quality of life by thinking this way. But when it comes to matters of the heart, the analogy starts to break down. Most people quickly discover the main difference between *homo sapiens* and other animals: our brains are meaning-making machines. Our brains continually seek to create a *story* to provide meaning to our experiences—especially when it comes to matters of the heart. As a result, we humans have a very difficult time having a sexual experience apart from asking what it "means."

Note that other mammals don't try to make meaning out of their experiences. Dogs don't ask, "Why is this happening to me?" Cats don't say to each other after sex, "I just really want to know that you love me for more than my body" or "I just don't feel you are as committed to this relationship as I am." In this sense, we're not like other animals.

So maybe we're not just animals. But we can frame our sexuality in another way just as dangerous: by taking the opposite extreme belief that we are angels. The angel idea denies the importance of the physical and that our sexuality helps makes us human. If animals are creatures with bodies but no souls, angels are creatures with a soul but no body.

It's true that some people identify as asexual. But for most of us sexual expression forms an important aspect of our humanity—and denying that it exists, seeking to repress it, or stuffing it deeper into our psyches creates the potential for greater damage. Christopher Ryan observes from his research:

> Nothing inspires murderous mayhem in human beings more reliably than sexual repression. Denied food, water, or freedom of movement, people will get desperate, and some may lash out at what they perceive as the source of their problems, albeit in a weakened state. But if expression of sexuality is thwarted, the human psyche tends to grow twisted into grotesque, enraged perversions of desire.[3]

We're not angels. Trying to live like an angel may be even more treacherous and destructive than trying to live like an animal. The carnage wrought by celibate priests in the recent Roman Catholic Church pedophile scandals shows how grotesque the perversions of repressed desire can become. In a Cathleen Falsani interview in the 1970s, Playboy founder Hugh Heffner reflected on his life with parents who thought they were angels:

> I was raised in a setting in which [sex] was for procreation only and the rest was sin. Our family was Puritan in a very real sense…Never hugged. There was absolutely no hugging or kissing in my family. There was a point in time when my mother, later in life, apologized to me for not being able to show affection. I said to her, "Mom, you couldn't have done it any better. And

because of the things you weren't able to do, it set me on a course that changed my life and the world."[4]

Heffner, of course, may have compensated by going toward the animal extreme.

The angels vs animals bifurcation plays out many ways in popular culture. Some circulate in memes on social media. One stereotype says, for instance, that teenage boys are animals and don't know how to control themselves; meanwhile, my little girl is an angel. *Rules to Date My Daughter* say things like:

1. You do not touch my daughter in front of me. You may glance at her, so long as you do not peer at anything below her neck. If you cannot keep your eyes or hands off of my daughter's body, I will remove them.

2. The following places are not appropriate for a date with my daughter: Places where there are beds, sofas, or anything softer than a wooden stool. Places where there are no parents, policemen, or nuns within eyesight. Places where there is darkness. Places where there is dancing, holding hands, or happiness. Places where the ambient temperature is warm enough to induce my daughter to wear shorts, tank tops, midriff T-shirts, or anything other than overalls, a sweater, and a goose down parka zipped up to her throat. Movies with a strong romantic or sexual theme are to be avoided. Movies, which feature chainsaws, are okay. Hockey games are okay. Old folk's homes are better.[5]

The truth is that teenage boys and teenage girls are neither animals nor angels. They're just human beings, and these kinds of caricatures don't help us in finding ways of talking about how we relate to each other as sexual beings.

Married Angels and Their Woes

When people who try to live like angels get married, trouble ensues. Sexless marriages are more common than most realize. Researchers estimate between 15% and 20% of married couples have "dead bedrooms."[6] In fact, Google searches for "sexless marriage" outnumber searches related to any other marital issue.[7] According to Dagmar Herzog, a leading researcher on the histories of sexuality and gender, the crisis of our day centers not on pre-marital sex but *post*-marital sex. She writes about marital sex and "its quality, its quantity…indeed its very existence" and says "Never before have so many Americans worried so much about whether they really even want sex at all."[8] (As the old joke goes, if you are against gay sex, you should be enthusiastically supportive of gay marriage!) In other words, marriage seems to kill sex. But for many, this isn't funny at all. The marriage expert Esther Perel notes:

> I have come to respect the power of deprivation for what it is. Our culture tends to minimize the importance of sex for the well-being of a couple. It is seen as optional…[W]hen sex is woefully lacking, and not by mutual agreement, it can leave a gap in an otherwise satisfying relationship that is unbearable.[9]

In my pastoral experience, I can think of numerous conversations with both husbands and wives who found themselves at their wits' end in a sexless marriage. One person confided to me their marriage frustration by referring to an episode of the Simpsons. In the episode, Lisa, has spurned the character Millhouse at every turn; yet when Millhouse gets a girlfriend, she becomes jealous and can't stop stalking him and his newfound love. Eventually, because of Lisa's stalking, the girlfriend leaves and Millhouse finds himself alone once again. In a moment of frustration and clarity, Millhouse says to Lisa, "You don't want me to be with you. You don't want me to be with someone else. How miserable do I have to be before you're happy?"[10]

The sexual needs of couples and how they should be resolved presents a complicated, sensitive topic and the scope of this book won't allow me to address all the nuances. That said, I have often left these conversations with the nagging feeling that maybe we should rethink some of our sexual ethics. Instead of saying stick it out in a sexless marriage, no matter how miserable, we could say: *Maybe me requiring my partner to be my exclusive expression of sexuality implies responsibility of effort on my part. I can't just restrict them without recourse or reciprocation. Otherwise, asking for monogamy is perhaps disingenuous and other options should be on the table.*

At least this is worth thinking about. People have sexual needs. We are neither angels nor animals. So, what are we?

Three Paradoxes about You and Me

In my experience, there are three paradoxes surrounding the human condition that shapes how we think, how we feel, and what we do when it comes to our sexuality.

We long for joy and delight but are fixated on pathology. In the same way that modern Western medicine and psychology historically has tended to focus on pathology, Western theology has tended to focus on sin and dysfunction rather than on what constitutes human thriving. For the most part, we don't find a lot of deep theological reflection on joy, delight, and pleasure. We don't usually have to justify our love of a piece of music, the appreciation of a sunset over the ocean, or the pleasure of a fabulously prepared meal. But for some reason, we feel we have to theologically justify the pleasure of sex. Human sexuality, in theological circles, seems always to be framed in terms of its pathology—how it goes wrong—rather than celebrating the joy of when it goes right. In fact, many of us who grew up in Evangelical circles find that we feel bad whenever we feel good. That's a problem.

We are both made in the Image of God and are deeply flawed. The deepest longings of our souls tend toward beauty and transcendence, but sometimes we get mired in what's wrong with us or what can go wrong with our actions. We human beings can be warped, selfish, self-absorbed—even our own worst enemies. We have an enormous capacity as humans for evil. (Our Reformed friends like to remind us of this truth perhaps a little too often.) But surely that's not the whole truth. Humans can also at times be powerful forces for good, for love, for human thriving, and redemption—living out a reflection of the image of God. At our best, we can make manifest to the world the glory of God within each of us. Both our negative and positive potentials are true, and we must hold them in tension. Nowhere is this paradox more evident than in human sexuality. When human sexuality's good, it's really good: it's loving, bonding, healing, and beautiful. And when it's bad, it can be really bad: it's dehumanizing, destructive, and traumatizing.

We crave both novelty and security. Deep within the human soul we have a longing for risk, adventure, novelty, and exploration. But also lying deep within we have a longing for safety, security, predictability, and permanence. You can see this paradox play out most clearly with young children as they play on a playground or a park. They run off to explore and then boomerang back to the safety of mom or dad's arms. But we do this as adults also. We live our lives with seasons of risk taking and seasons of nesting and grounding.[11] All living things hold this tension between growth and equilibrium. Organisms can't survive with too much change and chaos; likewise, stasis or prolonged equilibrium brings about the death of a living entity.

When it comes to intimate relationships, we long for transcendent experiences that take us to new places and new heights. We also long for faithful, consistent, and predictable partners. The Rom Com genre gives us the best of both of these worlds and that's why we love it so much: the characters meet someone new, exhilarating, and unique, and then they ride off into the sunset with the promise of permanence, security, and predictability. These stories scratch both the itch of novelty and security.

This tension can create complications in long-term relationships and marriages. Not too many movies deal with when the characters from the Rom Com come home from the honeymoon and have to paint the house, pay their taxes, or lance a boil. Esther Perel reflects on this challenge in her book, *Mating in Captivity:*

> For a lucky few, this [paradox] is barely a challenge. These couples can easily integrate cleaning the garage with rubbing each other's back. For them, there is no

dissonance between commitment and excitement, responsibility, and playfulness. They can buy a home and be naughty in it, too. They can be parents and still be lovers. In short, they're able to seamlessly meld the ordinary and the uncanny. But for the rest of us, seeking excitement in the same relationship in which we establish permanence is a tall order. Unfortunately, too many love stories develop in such a way that we sacrifice passion so as to achieve stability.[12]

Couples deal with this tension between novelty and security in a myriad of ways—some healthy and some not so healthy.

You. Me. Us.

A woman named Sharon who attended my church made her living as a marriage counselor. I asked her once about how her counseling practice had changed over the years. She mentioned the ways in which many couples were re-inventing marriage to make it work for them, but as she thought about it more, Sharon told me, "I do premarital counseling very differently now than I did twenty years ago." She explained that often she finds couples have unspoken beliefs about the definition of words like "monogamy," "cheating," and "faithful." With the advent of social media and the internet, our ability to make connections with people in faraway places has changed beyond anything that our ancestors could have imagined. Social media blurs the line between the forbidden and the merely nostalgic or harmless in the guise of ordinary exchanges. Infidelity used to be more intentional and less ambiguous when interactions were face to face in the bygone era of our parents. Pamela Haag observes that in our day, "The world isn't partitioned cataclysmically into Before and After by a fateful illicit kiss. In the cyber wonderland, infidelity has an almost imperceptibly thin razor's edge. It's the difference between a word or two in an email, or a flirtatious exchange that never even involves a touch."[13]

Sharon pushes couples to think through the question made famous by the Bill Clinton and Monica Lewinsky scandal of the 1990s—what precisely constitutes "sex"? As a result, Sharon asks her starry-eyed, engaged couples, "Tell me from this list what, if anything, do you consider 'cheating?'":

- Being Facebook friends with old boyfriends/girlfriends?
- Texting / phone calls / sliding into the DM's of old boyfriends / girlfriends?
- Going to dinner with someone else alone?
- Having romantic thoughts about someone else?
- Having a crush on someone else but not acting on it?
- Clubbing/dancing with someone else?
- Giving someone else a hug?
- Kissing someone else on the cheek?
- Kissing someone else on the lips?
- Talking about deep emotional and/or sexual things with other people on the internet, people you have never met and will likely never meet?
- Flirting with a cute stranger?
- Exchanging flirty texts with someone else?
- Writing a steamy fanfiction with someone else?
- Having sexy thoughts about someone else?
- Watching porn?
- Reading erotica?
- Masturbating?

Many may have never actually listed out or thought about these possibilities. Of course, this is not an exhaustive list, but Sharon facilitates these conversations to get couples to begin to think about how their sexuality affects or does not affect their partners. Sharon draws a Venn Diagram and explains how each person has their own individual sexuality, and then they have the sexuality that they share together:

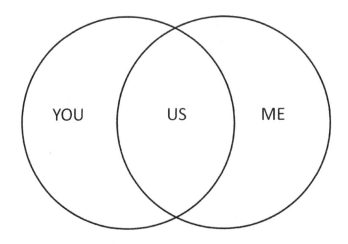

Some couples prefer the Venn Diagram to just be a circle: they believe there can be no sexual expression apart from each other. Others negotiate what will be exclusively "ours" and what will be "mine." She discovered that couples who did not come to an agreement about how their circles lined up were destined for trouble down the road. In our ultra-connected society, sexual expression has many, many new options and they come at us with surprising frequency.

The Monogamy Problem

Adultery remains the subject of fear, gossip, debates, and demonization. But however a couple chooses to define it, it's as old as the institution of marriage itself. Like marriage itself, however, the *reasons* for the distress around adultery have evolved. In previous eras, including the periods of the Old and New Testaments, adultery problematized society's norms because it destabilized families, clans, and financial systems (their physiological and safety needs). Historian Stephanie Coontz observes that oddly, for most of human history, adultery was often what people engaged in to *find* love. She writes, "Very often [romantic love and sexual infatuation] were seen as inappropriate when attached to marriage. Because marriage was a political, economic, and mercenary event, many people believed that true, uncontaminated love could only exist without it."[14]

That's the way it used to be. However, as "romantic" marriage arrived on the scene and as couples climbed further and further up Mount Maslow, adultery became problematic because it also devastated the higher belonging, esteem, and self-actualization needs (in addition to also frequently destroying the lower physiological and safety needs). In our culture, it's a distinctively agonizing experience to be "cheated on." For those near the top of Mount Maslow, it can feel unrecoverable. In fact, adultery remains the most cited reason why couples divorce. As the English playwright William Congreve once famously observed, "Heaven has no rage like love to hatred turned, nor hell no fury like a woman scorned."[15] Some of my most gut-wrenching moments as a pastor came sitting with a spouse who had discovered their partner cheating. I'll never forget sitting in my backyard with a pastor who worked for me after he discovered his wife was having an affair with a co-worker. The pain was so deep and raw that he lost all sense of decorum as he sobbed and cried out.

Despite how devastating adultery can be for the victimized partner, it's much more common than most realize.[16] Statistics can be hard to come by because, to nobody's surprise, people don't like to own up to the fact that they have cheated. Moreover, as discussed earlier, definitions of what exactly constitutes "cheating" can be slippery. Can forming a tight emotional bond with someone else (sometimes called "micro-cheating") be considered cheating? What about "emotional" affairs? Since the definition of "sex" and "cheating" can be so slippery, it can also change over time. I suggest this working definition of adultery: "Engaging in activities to which both you and your partner have not consented." In other words, participating in activities for which "we" have agreed, on the Venn diagram, were overlapping the "us only" territory.

Researchers of course remain interested in the question of who is having sexual intercourse with people to whom they are not married. Within that framework, some researchers on the *low-end* estimate that between 20% and 37% of us will cheat during our lifetimes.[17] In the *mid-range*, other researchers estimate that as high as 60% of men and 50% of women in the US have "reported sexual intercourse with someone who was not their spouse while they were married."[18]

Sexologist Shere Hite's research focused on couples who were married longer than five years in order to rule out the hormones and chemicals present in newlyweds (she looked at those on the "security" side of the tension rather than the "novelty" side of the tension). Her research found that no less than 70% of women and 75% of men who were married for more than five years have had extramarital sex.[19] These numbers are consistent whether one identifies as "Christian" or not. It should also be noted that these numbers reflect "sexual intercourse" *per se* and don't reflect the other ways that a person can violate the "us only" agreement of their Venn diagram: actions such as cyber-affairs, emotional affairs, or physical affairs that do not include sexual intercourse. All these statistics suggest that we have a serious monogamy crisis.

Some researchers look at these high infidelity rates and wonder if they reflect people's overall frame of mind about their marriages. In other words, perhaps we're witnessing a desperate surge of infidelity similar to "suicide by cop," in which some people opt for the option of "divorce by affair." Infidelity, then, becomes less about uncontrollable passion for another person and more about a way out of a marriage where another exit strategy seems difficult to find.

In the 1990s, I preached a sermon to my congregation entitled, *How to Affair Proof Your Marriage*. At the time I believed in the conventional wisdom that if people had stronger marriages, they wouldn't look outside their marriages to fill a void. I still believe this can be true for some marriages; but for many others, researchers are finding that infidelity does not correlate neatly with marital dysfunction.[20] Other more existential forces also tear at the fabric of monogamy: our loss of identity, our loss of freedom, and our mortality. Because we are not animals, our minds make meaning and narratives out of the experiences we have—including infidelity. Human nature makes us want to find a clear villain and a victim in the stories that we tell ourselves and to others. Often infidelity lends itself to a neat and tidy narrative with this villain and victim motif, and clear motives about why a person did a particular action. But infidelity isn't usually that simple. In the words of Esther Perel, "Infidelity may be ubiquitous, but the way we make meaning of it—how we define it, suffer from it, and talk about it—is ultimately linked to the particular time and place where the drama unfolds."[21] The actual reasons for infidelity are complex.

For some people, monogamy comes naturally and easily, but for others, monogamy can be a tremendous challenge. In one survey that was typical of respondents, the percentage of people who thought it was realistic to live monogamously for the entire duration of a marriage exceeded by far the percentage of people who actually succeed in doing it.[22] This suggests *we may believe in monogamy, but it doesn't seem to believe in us.* Anthropologists remind us about biological and evolutionary-psychological reasons for our failure to achieve monogamy.[23] Wednesday Martin writes:

[Monogamy is] a relatively recent, imperfect, species-wide compromise, a good enough way to find companionship and raise kids in our current ecological circumstances, in which we're far from extended family and without easy or high-quality childcare options. Some data suggest that long-term, committed relationships are good for us physically and emotionally. But there is also research indicating that marriage brings health benefits for men, not for women. And one sixteen-year longitudinal study of a representative sample of more than eleven thousand adults showed not only that marriage has little impact on health or happiness but that any positive effects of marriage are likely attributable to a more positive evaluation of one's life rather than improvement on concrete measures.[24]

From all this, we might conclude that if one struggles with monogamy, perhaps it's time for some grace. We are fighting against millions of years of biological and psychological evolution. If you don't struggle with monogamy, it's possible your character and moral fiber might be superior to others, and you are justified in your self-righteousness. However, according to the actual research, it's more likely that you just have a lower testosterone level than the average person.[25]

Some look at overwhelming infidelity rates and view them as a critique on monogamy itself. The link between monogamy and marriage played a critical role in bygone eras by assuring paternity—important in a patriarchal age—but some are shrugging monogamy off today as a vestigial organ like the appendix. Like divorce rates, adultery rates suggest to us that if a process or an institution has a very high failure rate, it might be time to look at the process or the institution itself rather than simply the character of the individuals involved—because all systems are perfectly designed to get the results they get. We need to understand *why* people commit adultery, not just castigate them for doing so.

It probably would be impossible to find someone in our day who would actually endorse adultery (now referred to as "unethical non-monogamy") as a good way to deal with the monogamy problem. But in both contemporary and historic cultures, we find different approaches to the role of monogamy in marriage. Since the agricultural revolution, people have used different methods to cope with the eternal tension between stability and novelty.

Ways People Deal with The Monogamy Problem

Wanting What You Have. For many, doing the hard work of adding novelty and doubling-down on their secure relationships seems the best option for dealing with the monogamy problem. Esther Perel explains that passion is like a fire—it needs both heat and air.[26] Consequently, in a counter-intuitive way, absence and longing (air) add key elements to passion in a relationship. Think of the old country/western song, "How Can I Miss You When You Won't Go Away?" When a person can get some distance from their partner and are able to see them as elusive and mysterious, in that space lies the erotic. Like so much of life, mystery may be not so much about traveling to new places as seeing what's familiar with new eyes.

Monogamy Agnosticism. Usually we think that when a partner proves unfaithful, the "innocent" partner will be devastated. But that's not always true. Sometimes offended spouses have generous clemency programs. For example, research in Great Britain found that a third of female respondents had already had an affair or were considering one. Of that third, almost half believed their husbands would forgive them for their unfaithfulness. And more than half said they would forgive their husbands if *they* were unfaithful.[27]

Julie came to me because she had confronted her husband about some text messages and emails, exchanges she found with one of his colleagues that seemed way too friendly. He confessed to an affair and swore to end it. But Julie wasn't sure what to do next. She came to me and told me, "I have a deep sense of shame and embarrassment about this, but I want to work it out with him. I'm afraid that everyone is going to think

I am weak or pathetic if I take him back." We could call this the "stand by your man" syndrome. It might seem inauthentic to others to try to work through the pain and save the marriage after an extra-marital affair.

While many people use hyperbole to talk about how they would respond if their partner cheated on them, in my experience, nobody knows how they will respond until they're in that situation. As it turns out, people may care about more than just sexual fidelity in their marriages. Sometimes those other facets of the marriage outweigh the infidelity. Julie told me, "Alan is a great dad. We have three kids together. He is a good provider. He is smart and funny, and I want to grow old with him. We have things we want to do together and places we want to go." She could have considered divorce. But facing the reality of only seeing her children half the time was the final factor in Julie's decision to forgive Alan and to try to rebuild trust. Later Julie told me, "In the ancient world, they build cities on top of cities. They just take the ruins from one and build the next one. I don't want my life to be like that. I want *this* city. I want *this* family."

I catch glimpses of Monogamy Agnosticism in some passing comments I overhear. "Everyone gets one free pass," I overheard a woman at Starbucks say to her friend. Another parishioner confided in me, "I'm not glad the affair happened, but it has really helped us communicate better what we want and need." Some people perform acts of downright willful incuriosity in their marriage as part of their Monogamy Agnosticism—they really don't want to know what their partner is doing. If they knew, they would have to pretend to care and deal with it; besides, they are fine with the ways things are. This attitude might be more common than we think.

Patty and James have been friends of mine for many years. They were coming up on their 35th year of marriage when James confessed to Patty that 20 years earlier, he had had a brief affair with someone in their church. Patty told me later, "I'm sure he felt a lot better getting it off his chest, but it was 20 years ago! What am I supposed to do with that now? I wish he would have never told me." For Monogamy Agnostics, infidelity can be an underwhelming crisis.

The Open Secret. Literary critic D.A. Miller has spelled out a psychological concept that helped me appreciate how infidelity often plays out in our world. Miller found it intriguing that in some literature, such as the book *David Copperfield* by Charles Dickens, "the secret is always known—and in some obscure sense known to be known [so that the] social function of secrecy is not to conceal knowledge or behavior so much as to conceal the knowledge of the knowledge."[28] Miller calls this concept *The Open Secret*—something we all know it to be true but which we all pretend that we don't know.

In France as well as many South American countries, it's common to treat non-monogamy (especially among men) with the careful practice of The Open Secret—"if you pretend you are monogamous in public, we will pretend to not know that you aren't." Our own country also had this ethos in the 1950s. Lip service to monogamy simultaneously created both public order and private spaces of freedom to do what people wanted. Alfred Kinsey's research during this supposedly conservative time revealed some very surprising insights. A total of 46% of women during this time had had extramarital encounters. Among those who reported encounters, 71% said they had "no difficulties with their marriages" because of it. Half said that their husbands knew about or suspected the affairs.[29] When social warriors clamor for a return to a 1950s ethos, they had better be careful what they wish for!

By the 1960s, researchers John Cuber and Peggy Harroff called these kinds of open secrets "adultery toleration." They reflected on couples who "evolved a rather elaborate mythology which enables most of them to live comfortably with the discrepancies between action and belief."[30] In more recent years, swingers seem to be the group who can "live comfortably with the discrepancies between action and belief." While stereotypes typify swingers as liberal, new-age, hippie types, research on their demographics reveal that most swingers are conservative both politically and religiously.[31] When we hear the news of a celebrity who has cheated or even someone in our circle of friends, we all act surprised. One recent tabloid headline about a celebrity cheater simply said, "What Was He Thinking?" But the truth is, affairs happen all the time, but we may feign surprise because we are playing our role as participants in the Open Secret.

Ethical Non-Monogamy or Polyamory. Since most of human history was patriarchal, most men who cheated practiced either the Open Secret or relied on Monogamy Agnosticism. Men would sleep around or have lovers on the side and there was not much women could do about it. A double standard, revealing itself, of course. Now as marriages become more and more egalitarian, however, sometimes both men and women seek to share their hearts and/or their bodies with others outside of their marriage, often with the full knowledge and consent of their partners.[32]

If you are thinking "I sure don't know anyone who is ethically non-monogamous or polyamorous," it's probably *not* because you don't. It's much more likely that someone in your life simply doesn't trust you with information about them that's not always socially acceptable. Recent research has shown that 10.7% of Americans have been polyamorous at some point in their lives and 16.8% of Americans desired to be polyamorous.[33] That number appears to be rapidly on the rise. In recent years, discussion of, and even support groups for, people in polyamorous relationships (defined as loving more than one person at a time) have grown as this option has come more and more into public consciousness.

For many married people, this topic hits a raw nerve. Privately, however, I am surprised at the number of people who confide in me that if ethical non-monogamy were socially acceptable, they would be open to the idea. Research indicates the younger a person is, the more open they are to ethical non-monogamy. Some speculate that younger generations who have grown up in an internet age may have a much larger "bandwidth" for complex moral input and relationships. Pamela Haag reflects:

> [Ethical non-monogamy or polyamory] subverts the strongest assumptions of the romantic marriage, its axioms that there is only one intimacy at a time, that romantic love isn't plural, and that jealousy renders multiple intimacies impossible. In envisioning a marital fidelity that's grounded not in the practice of monogamy but in ethical honesty, it's a staggering leap of faith, and anyone can be forgiven for their skepticism.[34]

Similarly, Carrie Jenkins notes that ethical non-monogamy threatens two core ideas in our culture: "paternity control through the sexual restriction of women and the conception of a romantic partner as one's private property. It strikes at the heart of the historic purpose of romantic love."[35]

Conventional wisdom says that ethical non-monogamy never works. Although research is in the developmental stages at this point, we can't simply dismiss it out of hand. Some research indicates that those who practice ethical non-monogamy are actually *healthier* and more content than their monogamous counterparts.[36] Both the space and the scope of this book don't allow me to make an adequate exploration of all the many nuances of ethical non-monogamy's attempt at dealing with the monogamy problem. However, I would remind my readers of my previous important form/function distinction. In thinking about a delicate topic such as ethical non-monogamy or polyamory, we should ask in dealing with different *forms* of marriage (especially ones that some may instinctively find "yucky") not just what they are, but how they *function* for people. Are people practicing these forms acting intentionally, in relational response to God and others, to promote overall well-being?[37] If so, how might that change our understanding of whether such practices may be permissible ethically?

CHAPTER 8

Blind to The Rich Possibility of Another Way of Being

"For stony limits cannot hold love out,
And what love can do, that dares love attempt."

–WILLIAM SHAKESPEARE, *ROMEO AND JULIET*–

"The most important thing about priorities...
is not intelligent analysis but courage:
Pick the future against the past;
Focus on an opportunity rather than on a problem;
Choose your own direction—rather
than climb on a bandwagon;
Aim high, aim for something that will make a difference,
rather than for something that is 'safe' and easy to do."

–PETER DRUCKER–

"To be the first to leave a crowd, to be the
first not to throw stones, is to run the risk of
becoming a target for the stone-throwers."

–RENÉ GIRARD–

MENTAL SOUNDTRACK

U2, "God, Part 2"
Ben Rector, "30,000 Feet"

During my many years of being a pastor, I officiated dozens of weddings. When I met with couples to work through logistics for their special day, I inevitably would ask them about the vows they planned. I usually needed to reassure the bride that the promise "to obey" was removed from the traditional wedding vows several decades ago. Sometimes I also found myself reassuring the couple that the "if anyone has objections to why this couple should not be married…" part is more Hollywood Rom Com and doesn't happen in contemporary weddings.[1]

Some couples choose to write their own wedding vows rather than use the traditional option. When this happens, I usually offer something along the lines of, "I think it would be beautiful and meaningful for you to write your own vows. However, let me give you my pitch as to why you should consider using both your own vows and traditional vows: This wedding is not just about you two. Yes, you are the ones who will be making the vows but there may be dozens, perhaps hundreds of people who will show up to support and encourage you in your journey. Many of these people stood in front of a congregation in a very similar fashion and as you repeat the traditional vows, your wedding will become tied to their wedding, in their minds. They will remember the vows they said, they will remember why they fell in love, and they will begin to re-commit themselves to the vows they made. Your wedding does not happen in a vacuum. Your story is tied to dozens, perhaps hundreds of other stories."

In recent years, some weddings I officiated revived the ancient Celtic tradition of handfasting in place of the unity candle. In the Celtic tradition, weddings included a ritual of binding the hands of the bride and groom with lengths of cloth, cord, or ropes as a symbol of their lasting union. We get our modern idiom for marriage, "tie the knot," from this ancient practice.

Weddings, like the marriages they create, are an amalgamation of old and new, ancient and modern, rich tradition and modern innovation. In some ways we are forever tied to marriage's past. However, our bonds to each other are often stronger than our traditions and this allows us to transcend what was to create new possibilities of what could be. Marriage at its best allows us to be tied to each other without being tied too tightly to the past. It allows us to separate the knot from the not any longer.

Religion has traditionally been about binding together. The word "religion" comes from two words: "lig" (from which we get our English word "ligament") which means to connect, to tie together, to unite, to bring everything together in wholeness; and the word "re"—which means "again." So, the original meaning of the word "religion" amounts to "connecting us together again." Or connecting us together with God, with creation, with each other. Religion helps us find again that vital binding makes us whole. Nadia Bolz-Weber elaborates on this biblical image:

> In ancient Greek, the root of demon means "to throw apart." That which causes us to fracture, to become less whole, is demonic…I like to think that when Jesus sent the disciples to cast out demons in his name, he intended for them to look with so much love upon those

who had become fractured that their neglected pieces returned to the center of their being.[2]

Religion is supposed to heal. However, sometimes it promotes conflict and selfishness rather than generosity and love. Certain teachings of religion, as we've seen, can prioritize one's own personal salvation over the well-being of others. Sometimes religion teaches people to fear, dehumanize, and judge others. When it does, religion strains or tears the ligaments of creation rather than strengthening the ties.

The church's history with marriage has been a mixed bag. Though this might surprise, for some of church history the Christian church was apathetic towards the institution of marriage. At its worst, the church's relationship with marriage has sometimes functioned to control and to preserve social order. At its best, the church has been at the forefront of re-thinking and re-imagining how marriage could be expressed in more loving and empowering forms. As we stumble into the future, my hope is that instead of "de-ligmenting" people through an alienating, ahistorical, and rules-based approach to marriage, we will pursue new, more loving forms of marriage. That we will allow people to "re-ligament" or knot their worlds back together again—to God, to others, and to the center of their own beings.

The Future of Marriage

Marriage in 100 years from now will undoubtedly look different from today. As we have seen, marriage evolves in both idea and practice. In preparation for this book, I spent about a year reading, thinking, and writing about love, sex, marriage, and Christian faith. The truth is, I could easily spend another two or three years and still not feel that I have a grasp on all the nuances of thinking about marriage, how it has changed, and how it is changing. As the cultural landscape shifts quickly, new research comes out all the time which can help us make wise, informed decisions.

Some trends seem to have some traction, however. If I were a leader of a faith community, I would particular attention to these:

- Singlehood and those who choose to never marry seem to be on a steady increase with no signs of slowing down. In the words of researcher Bella DePaulo, "Households with married couples are in the minority, with the majority of Americans living single. Americans will spend more of their lives single than married."[3]

- The divorce rate will probably continue to slowly drop— in part due to fewer people getting married, but also because people will discover new ways to stay married that would have been "deal breakers" in the past.

- Ethical non-monogamy and polyamory continues to grow in rapid popularity, especially among younger generations. With the possible exception of the full inclusion of LGBTQ+ people into communities of faith, ethical non-monogamy and polyamory will probably constitute the biggest ethical debate that faith leaders will have to tackle in the next 20 years.[4]

- Online relationships will continue to increase. Those of us not digital natives struggle to see the legitimacy of cyber-relationships. For those who participate in them, however, the processes of connecting with others may be different from before, but they are very real. One researcher explained, "Online relationships develop differently than offline relationships, progressing from the inside out."[5] Online relationships often allow for more psychological and emotional depth due to their reliance on verbal communication. Or more darkly, they can become mere fantasy projections in which the other person becomes a blank screen upon which we project our wishes of who we'd like them to be. In either case, cyber relationships won't go away and will increase in popularity.

Some readers may wonder after all this where my research has led me personally when it comes to relationships and marriage. I've been reluctant to state my own beliefs and experiences because decisions that people may make about their own relationships and marriages have so much to do with their own partners, familial support, social support, culture, access to financial resources, and a myriad of other factors. All these factors form the context from which people make wise decisions. In short, everyone's context differs from mine, and decisions that I have or have not made may be irrelevant to what's best for you. I also don't share my own journey into the future on the chance that readers may misconstrue that as a recommendation or the "right answer." I believe people must find the right answers for themselves. I will say this, though—I'm enough of a romantic to believe that love will overcome dysfunctional systems and structures we have inherited and find its expression. But I'm also enough of a realist to know that pioneers are the first ones to get shot. It will take a lot of courage for people to change their minds and practices in relation to such an important topic. They will need a lot of wisdom and support to help walk alongside them through it. Things on the marriage front will probably get ugly before they will get better.

The Future of YOUR Marriage

As I have told people about this project, they would sometimes ask me, "So, are you *for* marriage or *against* it?" I see an assumption beneath this question that I find unsettling: the idea that we must either agree to the rules of the institution of marriage *as it currently is* OR completely reject it. For those in difficult marriages, sometimes the choice presented them feels equally binary—either suck it up and quit whining, they're told, or throw in the towel. I like to think there's a third way, if only we have the imagination to see it.

There's an apocryphal story surrounding the first arrival of Spanish explorers in the Americas. As the story goes, Native Americans had never seen nor conceived of ships large enough to cross the Atlantic Ocean. Consequently, their sudden appearance would have been overwhelming. But the myth contends that because Native peoples had no category in their minds for ships like these, they literally could not see them. Their inability to understand led to a literal blindness, an inability to perceive and interpret visual data. In some sense, they couldn't "see" the ships, though they were right there.

The story probably isn't true, and we have no way to know for sure. But the real irony of the story comes down to this point: *we are blind to what it means to be blind*. Colonialism is, by definition, a blindness to the merits of another culture—the lack of imagination to see the rich possibility in another way of being. It was the Spaniards who were the truly blind ones and didn't know it.

A woman in one of my churches named Courtney grew up in a very conservative religious environment. Her life was sheltered and a bit naïve, but she married her college sweetheart and they had three kids together. All seemed well until her marriage fell apart. In the post-divorce counseling, her counselor asked her about her support systems. She spoke about her best friend Debbie and how rich their friendship had been. "I love her so, so much," Courtney said. The counselor felt as if there was something more there and began to probe, until she finally asked Courtney, "Are you *in* love with Debbie?"

Courtney told me that her gut response was, "No, of course not, because I am not gay." It took a few days for Courtney to realize that what she was seeing on the horizon were tall ships. Because of her upbringing, she had a failure of imagination for what could be. She was blind to the rich possibility of another way of being: maybe she *was* gay, though that had seemed unthinkable.

Freedom to be often can be not so much an outward struggle as an inward struggle. Eric Fromm wrote some 50 years ago, "Although man [sic] has rid himself of old enemies of freedom, new enemies of a different nature have arisen; enemies which are not essentially external restraints, but internal factors blocking the full realization of the freedom of personality."[6]

My hope and prayer for you? That you will have both eyes to see and courage to act. May you be audacious and ambitious in the way you love. May you navigate the difficult waters of work, career, free time, family life, sex, and community in order to live large into your relationships. May you take responsibility for your own contentment. More than anything else, may you be a conduit of God's grace by acting intentionally, in relational response to God and others, to promote overall well-being.

I hope the reflection and principles of this book provide a compass that will enable you to create maps to guide you through the different seasons of your relationships, and to create yet unimagined forms of marriage that will lead to overall well-being of yourself and others. Here's the guiding principles we talked about:

Marriage as a Social Construct - Marriage has been changing and evolving since the Agricultural Revolution and will continue to change and evolve. Your marriage should change and evolve also. Social constructs may be real, but they are also dynamic.

Form Follows Function - The *form* a marriage takes should be a secondary consideration to the *function* of a marriage: that purpose is to love ("To act intentionally, in relational response to God and others, to promote overall well-being").

High Altitudes Can Be Treacherous in a Marriage - Freighting a marriage with higher and higher expectations as we climb Mount Maslow requires more and more oxygen to survive. Proceed with caution.

Pick the Form Best Suited for Your Marriage from a Buffet Menu - Unexamined cultural beliefs and unspoken assumptions should not be the foundation for expectations in your relationship; rather, what works for your unique personalities, experiences, and life stage should form the basis of your decision making.

Clear is Kind; Unclear is Unkind - Partners should communicate right upfront about whatever expectations they have regarding the various aspects of Mount Maslow and the mutual fulfillment of needs, knowing these expectations will change with time and will need to be frequently revisited.

Purity Culture is Toxic and Sex is Vital - For most people, sexual expression encompasses a vital part of being human and provides a means to joy, delight, and well-being—both for themselves and their partners. It shouldn't be discounted in a marriage or destroyed by purity culture.

I believe that new, brilliant and creative leaders will arise to lead healthy expressions of marriage into the future, helping us to abandon the sacrilegious chains of purity culture and other vestiges of patriarchal baggage from the past. Marriage is worth saving. I imagine that brave souls will soon begin to re-define marriage by embracing unique and unimaginable *forms* that follow the intended *function* of this ancient institution. In this sense, they will be like Jesus: not attempting to abolish the Law, but to fulfill its original intention: Love.[7]

"To love or have loved, that is enough.
Ask nothing further. There is no other pearl
to be found in the dark folds of life."

–VICTOR HUGO, *LES MISÉRABLES*–

Notes

Introduction: Marriage is a Wonderful Institution, But Who Wants to Live in an Institution?

1. This 50% statistic that is thrown around a lot is, obviously, much more nuanced. Many variables including age, race, economic status, education, IQ, religious beliefs, and whether is it one's first, second, or subsequent marriage are contributing factors. What makes divorce rates difficult to measure is the methodology employed. Since researchers do not have a crystal ball to know how a marriage will end, they will often take the number of marriages per thousand in a year and divide that by the number of divorces per thousand in a year. However, the number of people who are getting married has been in a steady decline for the last 30 years, so the results are a little misleading. Given that caveat, today the divorce rate is down from the all-time high of the early 1980s but still it is predicted that a little less than 50% of all marriages will end in divorce or separation (41% of first marriages, 60% of second marriages, and 73% of third marriages). Cf. "National Center for Health Statistics," Center for Disease Control and Prevention, accessed April 17, 2022, https://www.cdc.gov/nchs/fastats/marriage-divorce.htm.

2. Stephanie Coontz, *Marriage, a History: From Obedience to Intimacy or How Love Conquered Marriage* (New York: Viking, 2005), 173. – The average duration of marriage increased from about fifteen to twenty years in preindustrial Europe to about thirty-five years in 1900. cf. Roderick Phillips, *Putting Asunder: A History of Divorce in Western Society* (Cambridge, UK: Cambridge University Press, 1988), 393.

3. Wednesday Martin, *Untrue: Why Nearly Everything We Believe About Women, Lust, and Infidelity is Wrong and How the New Science Can Set Us Free* (New York: Little, Brown Spark, 2018), 39.

4. "Groucho Marx > Quotes > Quotable Quote," Good Reads, accessed March 31, 2022, https://www.goodreads.com/quotes/158923-marriage-is-a-wonderful-institution-but-who-wants-to-live-in.

5. "As U.S. marriage rate hovers at 50%, education gap in marital status widens," Pew Research Center, accessed April 13, 2022, https://www.pewresearch.org/fact-tank/2017/09/14/as-u-s-marriage-rate-hovers-at-50-education-gap-in-marital-status-widens/.

6. Ibid.

7. Martin, *Untrue*, 39.

8. Pamela Smock, "The Wax and Wane of Marriage: Prospect for Marriage in the 21st Century." *Journal of Marriage and Family* 66, no. 4 (2004): 966-73.

9. Pamela Haag, *Marriage Confidential: Love in the Post-Romantic Age* (New York: Harper Perennial, 2011), 13.

10. Jennifer Glass and Philip Levchak, "Red States, Blue States, and Divorce: Understanding the Impact of Conservative Protestantism on Regional Variation in Divorce Rates," *American Journal of Sociology* 119, no. 4 (January 2014), https://doi.org/10.1086/674703.

11. Mark Gungor, *Mark Gungor* (blog), accessed April 17, 2022, https://markgungor.com/.

12. "Red states, blue states, and divorce: Understanding the impact of conservative protestantism on regional variation in divorce rates," The University of Texas, accessed May 2, 2022, https://sites.utexas.edu/contemporaryfamilies/2014/01/16/impact-of-conservative-protestantism-on-regional-divorce-rates/.

13. The original source of this quote is in question. W. Edwards Deming was known to say it but there seems to be a good chance Paul Batalden altered a quote from Arthur Jones. It has now become a truism in organizational leadership. Cf. "Every system is perfectly designed to get the results it gets," The Deming Institute, accessed May 2, 2022, https://deming.org/quotes/10141/.

14. Carrie Jenkins, *What Love is and What It Could Be* (New York: Basic Books, 2017), 167.

15. Jonathan Haidt, *The Righteous Mind: Why Good People Are Divided by Politics and Religion* (New York: Vintage Books, 2012), 3-32.

16. Taylor Swift, *You Need to Calm Down,* Republic Records, 2019, compact disc.

Chapter 1: Trapped in History

1. Christopher Ryan and Cacilda Jetha, *Sex at Dawn: How We Mate, Why We Stray, and What It Means for Modern Relationships* (New York: Harper Perennial, 2010), 246; Robert Wright, *The Moral Animal: Why We Are, the Way We Are: The New Science of Evolutionary Psychology* (New York: Vintage Books, 1994), 49-69.

2. Ryan and Jetha, *Sex at Dawn,* 79ff and Wright, *The Moral Animal,* 67ff.

3. Wright, *The Moral Animal,* 93ff.

4. "Early Agriculture and The Rise Of Civilization," Encylopedia.com, accessed January 18, 2022, https://www.encyclopedia.com/science/encyclopedias-almanacs-transcripts-and-maps/early-agriculture-and-rise-civilization.

5. Jared Diamond, "The Worst Mistake in the History of the Human Race," *Discover Magazine,* April 30, 1999. accessed December 17, 2021, https://www.discovermagazine.com/planet-earth/the-worst-mistake-in-the-history-of-the-human-race.

6. Agustin Fuentes, *Race, Monogamy, and Other Lies They Told You: Busting Myths About Human Nature* (Berkeley: University of California Press, 2012), 178.

7. Genesis 3:16-19

8. Deuteronomy 25:5-10

9. Deuteronomy 22:13-21

10. Deuteronomy 22:28-29

11. Walter Brueggemann, "What Scripture Has to Say," *Outreach,* September 4, 2022, accessed September 23, 2022, https://outreach.faith/2022/09/walter-brueggemann-how-to-read-the-bible-on-homosexuality/.

12. While it is an ongoing debate among biblical scholars as to whether the couple was married or not (or whether the book is a collection of poems about different couples), the consensus seems to be that they were unmarried based on their living arrangements (cf. Songs of Songs 1:4, 2:14, 3:4, 5:2, and 8:2).

13. Of course, I know exactly what they mean. This is a cultural and political argument, not a theological or biblical one. As Kristin Kobes Du Mez so accurately observes, "Despite evangelicals' frequent claims that the Bible is the source of their social and political commitments, evangelicalism must be seen as a cultural and political movement rather than as a community defined chiefly by its theology." Kristin Kobes Du Mez, *Jesus and John Wayne: How White Evangelicals Corrupted a Faith and Fractured a Nation* (New York: Liveright Publishing, 2020), 297-98.

14. Deuteronomy 24:1

15. Exodus 21:10-11

16. Another rule they came up with was if a husband was unemployed, he had to at least make the offer of physical intimacy every night, seven nights a week, or his wife could divorce him. It makes one wonder if there was an epidemic of unemployment among the rabbis of Ancient Israel.

17. Matthew 1:19

18. Matthew 19:1-12

19. Luke 9:60

20. Luke 8:19-21

21. John 19:25–27

22. Luke 14:26, New Living Translation

23. Cf. Matthew 13:44-46

24. Matthew 19:3

25. Mark 6:18

26. Matthew 19:8

27. Matthew 19:9

28. 1 Corinthians 7:25-27; see also 1 Corinthians 7:38

29. See 1 Corinthians 7:10 and 1 Corinthians 7:12

30. See Ephesians 5:21-6:9

31. Galatians 3:26-28; NIV

32. Mark 2:27

33. Johannes Quasten and Joseph C. Plumpe, *Tertullian Treatises on Marriage and Remarriage* (New York: Newman, 1951), 35-45.

34. Stephanie Coontz, "Family Values, Social Reciprocity, and Christianity," in *Human Families: Identities, Relationships, and Responsibilities*, ed. Jacob M. Kohlhaas and Mary M. Doyle Roche, College Theology Society Annual, vol 66. (Maryknoll, NY: Orbis Books, 2021).

35. "St. Augustine was a womanizer, gambler and critic of the virtues. He fathered a son from a mistress before he turned twenty, lived with her for 10 years out of wedlock, and then dumped her so he could marry a socialite. Even after he entered a monastery he used to pray, 'Give me chastity, but not yet!' Some scholars believe that St. Augustine was gay. This assertion is based in part on a passage from *Confessions* about a man he knew as youth. 'I felt that his soul and mine were 'one soul in two bodies' and therefore life without him was horrible. I hated to live as half of a life.' After the man's death Augustine said he contemplated suicide but 'I feared to die, lest he should die wholly whom I had loved so greatly.' Despite his hedonistic ways, St. Augustine was drawn to religious cults that preached self-denial." ("St. Augustine: His Life, Confessions and Teachings," Facts and Details, accessed January 12, 2022, https://factsanddetails.com/world/cat55/sub391/item1411.html#:~:text=young%20Augustine%3F-,St.,chastity%2C%20but%20not%20yet!%E2%80%9D).

36. St. Augustine, "De Bono Coniugali," in *St. Augustine, Treatises on Marriage and Other Subjects,* trans. Charles T. Wilcox (Washington, DC: Catholic University of America Press, 1999) 9:9.

37. Coontz, *Marriage: A History*, 88-103.

38. Charles Reid Jr., *Power over the Body, Equality in the Family: Rights and Domestic Relations in Medieval Canon Law* (Grand Rapids, MI: Eerdmans, 2004), 200–210; Dale B. Martin, *Sex and the Single Savior* (Louisville, KY: Westminster John Knox Press, 2006).

Chapter 2: The Disney Princess/Rom-Com Industrial Complex: The Rise of Romantic Marriage

1. Coontz, *Marriage, a History*, 146.

2. Ibid, 148.

3. Ibid, 146.

4. Ibid, 229.

5. Peer Vos, *Someday My Prince Will Come.* Wyncote Music, 1964, compact disc.

6. Mandy Len Catron, "What You Lose When You Gain a Spouse," *The Atlantic Magazine*, July 2, 2019, accessed March 18, 2022, https://www.theatlantic.com/family/archive/2019/07/case-against-marriage/591973/.

7. Plato, *The Symposium,* trans. Christopher Gill (London: Penguin Books, 1999), 23-26.

8. Kimberly Johnson, & Bjarne Holmes, "Contradictory Messages: A Content Analysis of Hollywood-Produced Romantic Comedy Feature Films," *Communication Quarterly* 57, no. 3 (August 2009): 352-373.

9. Chris Donaghue, *Sex Outside the Lines: Authentic Sexuality in a Sexually Dysfunctional Culture* (Dallas: BenBella Books, 2015), 89.

10. Haag, *Marriage Confidential,* 145.

11. Ibid.

12. Loren Baritz, *The Good Life: The Meaning of Success for the American Middle Class* (New York: Knopf, 1988), 204.

13. "May Appoints Minister to Tackle Loneliness Issues Raised by Jo Cox," The Guardian, accessed November 28, 2021, https://www.theguardian.com/society/2018/jan/16/may-appoints-minister-tackle-loneliness-issues-raised-jo-cox.

14. "Work and the Loneliness Epidemic," Harvard Business Review, accessed November 28, 2021, https://hbr.org/2017/09/work-and-the-loneliness-epidemic.

15. Julianne Holt-Lunstad, Timothy B. Smith, and J. Bradley Layton, "Social Relationships and Mortality Risk: A Meta-analytic Review," *PLOS Medicine* (July 27, 2010), https://doi.org/10.1371/journal.pmed.1000316.

16. Elizabeth Brake, *Minimizing Marriage: Marriage, Morality, and the Law* (New York: Oxford University Press, 2012).

17. Jenkins, *What Love is and What it Could Be,* 142.

18. Coontz, *Marriage: A History,* 159.

19. Uwe Hartmann, "Sigmund Freud and His Impact on Our Understanding of Male Sexual Dysfunction," *Journal of Sexual Medicine* 6, no. 8 (August 1, 2009): 2332-39, https://www.jsm.jsexmed.org/article/S1743-6095(15)32613-8/fulltext.

20. Ibid.

21. Jenkins, *What Love is and What it Could Be,* 139.

22. Ibid.

23. Wright, *The Moral Animal,* 29-30.

24. Kobes Du Mez, *Jesus and John Wayne,* 277-278.

25. Jenkins, *What Love is and What it Could Be,* 112.

26. Cf. John 13:34, John 10:25-37, and Matthew 25:31-46 – in fact, just read any of the Gospels (especially Luke's) and it is abundantly clear what the central message of Jesus was: he came to bring a new world order (The Kingdom of God). For some, it may be shocking to discover how little Jesus talks about sex per se. Jesus seemed more interested in more general frameworks and principles of how we treated each other than specific actions. In other words, as noted earlier, Jesus did not have a lot of tolerance for de-ontological ethics.

27. Coontz, *Marriage: A History,* 168.

28. Nadia Bolz-Weber, *Shameless: A Sexual Reformation* (New York: Crown Publishing, 2019), 26.

29. There are, of course, exceptions to this myopic approach: World Vision and Compassion International are good examples of Evangelicals interest in poverty. (Although, it is worth nothing that generally their focus is poverty in the developing world, not domestic poverty issues). Additionally, most of the faith-based work with the homeless and the hungry in the US is done by Mainline, not Evangelical Christians. The one exception to this generalization is the Salvation Army. But even the Salvation Army gets most of its financial support from outside of the Evangelical world.

30. I am aware that abortion arose as an issue for the Religious Right as a result of Federal Government interference with racial segregation at Christian Universities in the 1970s; [cf. Randall Balmer, *Bad Faith: Race and The Rise of the Religious Right* (Grand Rapids: Eerdmans), 2022.] however, the discussion of race is outside the scope of this book. What is interesting to me is how quick and easy abortion was picked up as a proxy issue because of the sexual undertones involved.

31. St. Junia United Methodist Church, Facebook, May 20, 2019, https://www.facebook.com/SaintJunia/posts/to-answer-your-questions-yes-our-own-dave-barnhart-pastor-at-saint-junia-united-/2196128013775085/.

32. Nicholas Kristoff, "How Can This Be 'Pro-Life'?: Three Questions for Abortion Opponents Celebrating The End of Roe v. Wade," accessed July 1, 2022, https://nickkristof.substack.com/p/how-can-this-be-pro-life?sd=pf.

33. "Southern Baptist Convention Resolutions on Abortion," *Johnston's Archive,* accessed September 23, 2022, https://www.johnstonsarchive.net/baptist/sbcabres.html.

34. Coontz, *Marriage: A History,* 181.

35. Kobes Du Mez, *Jesus and John Wayne,* 302-03.

Chapter 3: The Implosion and The Possibility

1. Natalia Sarkisian and Naomi Gerstel, "Does Singlehood Isolate or Integrate? Examining the Link Between Marital Status and Ties to Kin, Friends, and Neighbors," *Journal of Social and Personal Relationships* 33, issue 3 (2016): 361-84, https://doi.org/10.1177/0265407515597564.

2. Mark Richard Purves, "Marriage in the Short Stories of Chekhov." *CLCWeb: Comparative Literature and Culture* 16, no. 3 (2014), https://doi.org/10.7771/1481-4374.2454.

3. Andrew J. Cherlin, *The Marriage-Go-Round: The State of Marriage and The Family in America Today* (New York: Vintage Books, 2009), 11-12.

4. Ibid, 171-72.

5. Paul Amato, "Good Enough Marriages: Parental Discord, Divorce, and Children's Well Being," *Virginia Journal of Social Policy and the Law* 9 (2002): 71-94.

6. Brooke Adams, "Holy Matrimony! Utah is the Place for Couples: Marriage: Utahns Lead the Nation," *Salt Lake Tribune*, March 14, 2003.

7. Bella DePaulo, "Living Single: Lightening Up Those Dark, Dopey Myths," in *The Dark Side of Personal Relationships II,* eds. William R. Cupach and Brian H. Spitzberg, (New York: Routledge, 2011), 409-39. Another aspect to the relationship between marriage and happiness is what marriage researcher Eli Finkel calls, "High Altitude Marriages." Finkel argues that some marriages, with the proper amount of time and energy investment, can be a source of happiness and well-being. Finkel's concepts and how they fit within the broader framework of re-thinking romantic marriage is discuss in detail in chapter 5 of this book.

8. Catron, "What You Lose When You Gain a Spouse"

9. Sarkisian and Gerstel, "Does Singlehood Isolate or Integrate?"

10. Ibid. Sarkisian and Gerstel found that, generally, these trends couldn't be explained away by structural differences in the lives of married versus unmarried people. The patters are consistent across racial groups and even when researchers control for age and socioeconomic status. In other words, it is not the circumstances of married life that isolate people, it is the institution of marriage itself.

11. Amy Gahran has done some interesting research on people who have intentionally defied this social norm in her book, *Stepping off The Relationship Escalator: Uncommon Love and Life* (Boulder, CO: Off the Escalator Enterprises, LLC, 2017).

12. "Making Room: Housing for a Changing America," AARP, accessed March 4, 2022, https://www.aarp.org/content/dam/aarp/livable-communities/livable-documents/documents-2019/making-room-web-spreads-010819.pdf.

13. Quoted in "The So-What View of Marriage," editorial, *Omaha World Herald*, April 24, 2000.

14. "Enjoli Perfume 'I'm A Woman' Commercial (1979)," Youtube video, 0:34, posted by Bionic Disco, https://www.youtube.com/watch?v=N_kzJ-f5C9U&ab_channel=BionicDisco.

15. Haag, *Marriage Confidential*, 48.

16. As nice of a thought as this may be, as noted earlier, research shows exactly the opposite: marriage generally tends to make us MORE selfish and MORE self-absorbed, not less.

17. Blaine Harden, "Bible Belt Couples 'Put Asunder' More, Despite New Efforts," *New York Times,* May 21, 2001.

18. David Brooks, "The Elusive Altar," *New York Times,* January 18, 2007.

19. Haag, *Marriage Confidential,* 14.

20. "I Do...For Now. UK Muslims Revive Temporary Marriages," BBC News, accessed June 3, 2020, https://www.bbc.com/news/uk-22354201.

21. "Bavarian Politician Proposes Seven-Year Limit on Marriage," DW Akademie, accessed September 23, 2022, https://www.dw.com/en/bavarian-politician-proposes-seven-year-limit-on-marriage/a-2790031.

22. Erin McDowell, "There's Been a 62% Spike in People Getting Prenups, And Experts Say It's Being Driven by Millennials," Business Insider, accessed June 4, 2022, https://www.businessinsider.com/millennials-are-driving-an-increase-in-prenuptial-agreements-2019-8.

23. Jonathon Gottschall, *The Story Paradox: How Our Love of Storytelling Builds Societies and Tears Them Down* (New York: Basic Books, 2021), 108-10.

24. Marilyn Gardner, "A Quiet Revolution in Support of Marriage," *The Christian Science Monitor* (June 30, 2000): 2.

25. Kathleen Gerson, "Moral Dilemmas, Moral Strategies, and The Transformation of Gender," *Gender and Society* 16, no. 1 (February 2002): 8-28.

26. Gillian Bowditch, "Mr. Right? That Can Be Arranged," *Sunday Times,* November 18, 2007.

An interesting discussion on modern arranged marriage can also be found at: "New York Magazine's Sex Lives: The Case for Arranged Marriage," The Cut, accessed April 4, 2022, https://www.thecut.com/2016/06/case-for-arranged-marriage.html.

27. Danielle Page, "Why You Should Treat Marriage More Like a Business: Lessons in Making a Marriage Last From The Matchmakers Behind Married At First Sight," Better by Today, June 30, 2017, accessed September 23, 2022, https://www.nbcnews.com/better/pop-culture/why-you-should-treat-marriage-more-business-ncna778551.

28. Raoul Felder, *Raoul Felder, Esq.* (blog), accessed February 3, 2022, https://www.raoulfelder.com.

29. Bolz-Weber, *Shameless,* 5.

30. "Sex and Employment: New Hiring Law Seen Bringing More Jobs, Benefits for Women," *Wall Street Journal,* January 22, 1965.

31. Brian McLaren, *A New Kind of Christianity: Ten Questions That Are Transforming the Faith* (New York: HarperOne, 2010), 122.

Chapter 4: Form Follows Function

1. Louis H. Sullivan, "The Tall Office Building Artistically Considered," *Lippincott Magazine,* March 1896, 6.

2. Thomas J. Oord, *Pluriform Love: An Open and Relational Theology of Well-Being* (Nampa, ID: SacraSage Press, 2022), 28.

3. A legal and ethical clarification – most states have mandatory reporting laws for counselors and clergy when it comes to the sexual abuse of a minor. I told Jennifer that I was bound by state law to report the incident so she might as well report it to the police also.

4. Mark 2:27

5. 2 Timothy 3:5

6. Luke 10:37

7. Luke 10:36

8. Luke 9:23

9. I am indebted to the insights from Resa Aslan's book, "Zealot" for another helpful and beautiful way of interpreting this passage. Aslan suggests that taking up one's cross in order to follow Jesus had less to do with self-sacrifice (a metaphorical interpretation) and more to do with a literal response that the Roman Empire would have to those who would follow in the footsteps of the Galilean rabbi who pushed back against the power and control of empires. In either interpretation, the principle remains the same—Jesus was suggesting that we adopt the same habits and attitudes that he demonstrated on a daily basis: like resisting oppressive power against the poor and marginalized. [cf. Resa Aslan, *Zealot: The Life and Times of Jesus of Nazareth* (New York: Random House, 2014).] I am also indebted to my friend Bernie Pollack for suggesting the book to me!

10. Ronald F. Duska, *Moral Development: A Guide to Piaget and Kohlberg* (New York: Paulist Press, 1975).

11. 1 Corinthians 13:11

12. Cf. "Section: Human Sexuality and Marriage," Church of the Nazarene Manual 2017-2021, accessed January 15, 2022, https://2017.manual.nazarene.org/section/human-sexuality-and-marriage/ – While it is outside the scope of this book to go line by line through the Church of the Nazarene's statement on human sexuality, the statement on polygamy and polyandry as well as the statements on "unmarried sexual intercourse" excludes a large number of people in the Hebrew Scriptures as well as many people in church history.

13. There are certain specific sexual activities that the Old Testament prohibits outright: incest, sex with animals, rape, sex with a woman during her menstrual cycle, sex with people of the same gender, etc. Some of these prohibitions make a lot of sense to our modern ears as they lack consent, take advantage of others, or do not promote overall well-being in ourselves or our communities. However, some of these prohibitions were reflections of the culture of the Ancient Near East and while they had meaning to the overall well-being of their communities during that particular time, they lack the same weight in our day. As such, it requires discernment and wisdom to be able to recognize the larger question for sexual ethics—"How do my actions promote relational response to God and others, to promote overall well-being?"

14. Matthew 5:17

15. Exodus 20:13

16. Matthew 5:21-22

17. Mark 12:31

18. John 15:13

19. Philemon 16

20. Galatians 3:28

21. I do not mean to imply that either slavery is somehow ended in our world or that somehow the effects of slavery in my country magically disappeared on Juneteenth. There is much, much work left undone. The point is simply that, as slow as it is, we have made progress and are (too slowly) moving forward since the days of the biblical writers.

Chapter 5: I Kissed Romantic Marriage Goodbye

1. Max Ehrenfreund, "The One Supreme Court Paragraph On Love That Gay Marriage Supporters Will Never Forget," Washington Post, June 26, 2015, https://www.washingtonpost.com/news/wonk/wp/2015/06/26/the-one-supreme-court-paragraph-on-love-that-gay-marriage-supporters-will-never-forget/.

2. Jenkins, *What Love is and What it Could Be,* 126-27.

3. The irony for Kilgore is that romantic comedies have given him the impression that stalking is the way to a woman's heart.

4. If you did not grow up in a church youth group, winkum resembled a kind of musical chairs except you tried to "steal" someone of the opposite sex by winking at them. It was popular because it allowed church teenagers to express affection in a controlled environment. Chubby Bunny was a game in which teenagers would see who could stuff their mouths with the most marshmallows while still being able to say the words, "chubby bunny." Chewing and swallowing was not allowed. Choking and vomiting was not uncommon when the marshmallow count would get too high. In the 1980s and 1990s wild west of youth ministry, the game was very popular. However, in 1999 a girl choked to death playing the game and the game is now barred from most youth groups. Cf. - "Chubby Bunny Marshmallows Choking Death," Snopes, accessed May 3, 2022, https://www.snopes.com/fact-check/chubby-bunny-death/

5. cf. Joshua Harris, *I Kissed Dating Goodbye* (Colorado Springs: Multnomah Books, 1997). Kristin Kobes Du Mez eloquently recounts this period in Evangelical history in *Jesus and John Wayne,* 169-72.

6. Beginning in 2016, Josh Harris began to retract and apologize for the content of his influential book and directed his publishing company to discontinue publishing it. In 2019, Harris posted on his Instagram account that he and his wife Shannon were separating. Later that year, Harris announced that he was no longer a Christian.

Parke, Caleb, "Well-known Christian Author, Purity Advocate, Renounces His Faith: 'I Hope You Can Forgive Me'," Fox News, accessed March 24, 2022, https://www.foxnews.com/faith-values/christian-author-joshua-harris-kissed-dating-goodbye-faith.

7. cf. Matthew 9:16-17

8. A. H. Maslow, "A Theory of Human Motivation," *Psychological Review* 50, no. 4 (1943): 370–96, https://doi.org/10.1037/h0054346.

9. Eli J. Finkel, *The All-or-Nothing Marriage: How The Best Marriages Work* (New York: Dutton, 2017), x.

10. Pamela Druckerman, *Lust in Translation: Infidelity from Tokyo to Tennessee* (New York: Penguin Books, 2007), 273.

11. Finkel, *The All or Nothing Marriage,* 12.

12. W.M. Pinsof, "The Death of 'Till Death Us Do Part': The Transformation of Pair-Bonding in The 20th Century," *Family Processes* 41, (2002): 135–57.

13. P. Uhlenberg, "Death and the family," *Journal of Family History* 5 (1980): 313–20.

14. Elizabeth Gilbert, *Eat Pray Love: One Woman's Search for Everything Across Italy, India, and Indonesia* (New York: Riverhead Books, 2006), 13.

15. Bruce Headey, Ruut Veenhoven, and Alex Wearing, "Top-Down Versus Bottom-Up Theories of Subjective Well-Being," *Social Indicators Research* 24, (1991): 81–100, https://doi.org/10.1007/BF00292652.

16. Maslow, "A Theory of Human Motivation," 99.

17. Finkel, *The All or Nothing Marriage,* 22.

18. Taylor Swift, "Blank Space," written with Martin Max and Johan Shellback, track 2 on *1989,* Big Machine Records, 2014, compact disc.

19. *Sideways,* directed by Alexander Payne (2004; Los Angeles, CA: Fox Searchlight Pictures, 2005), DVD. The clip in its full context can be viewed here: https://www.youtube.com/watch?v=QCS1Gnwbtp0&ab_channel=Movieclips.

Chapter 6: Clear is Kind. Unclear is Unkind.

1. Alain de Button, *How to Think More About Sex* (New York: Picador, 2012), 152.

2. Tim Ferris, *Tools of Titans: The Tactics, Routines, and Habits of Billionaires, Icons, and World-Class Performers* (Boston: Houghton Mifflin Harcourt, 2017), 268.

3. Todd Rose, *The End of Average: How We Succeed in a World That Values Sameness* (New York: HarperOne, 2015), 10.

4. Gary Chapman, *The Five Love Languages: The Secret to Love That Lasts* (Chicago: Northfield, 2015).

5. Ironically, parenthood seems to be the one of the strongest bonds for many to get and stay married. It seems obvious to everyone that parenthood is much easier as a team sport than as a solo endeavor.

6. This is based on the poem by Jack Gilbert:

> *"Everyone forgets that Icarus also flew.*
> *It's the same when love comes to an end,*
> *or the marriage fails and people say*
> *they knew it was a mistake, that everybody*
> *said it would never work. That she was*
> *old enough to know better. But anything*
> *worth doing is worth doing badly.*
> *Like being there by that summer ocean*
> *on the other side of the island while*
> *love was fading out of her, the stars*
> *burning so extravagantly those nights that*
> *anyone could tell you they would never last.*
> *Every morning she was asleep in my bed*
> *like a visitation, the gentleness in her*
> *like antelope standing in the dawn mist.*
> *Each afternoon I watched her coming back*
> *through the hot stony field after swimming,*
> *the sea light behind her and the huge sky*
> *on the other side of that. Listened to her*
> *while we ate lunch. How can they say*
> *the marriage failed? Like the people who*
> *came back from Provence (when it was Provence)*
> *and said it was pretty but the food was greasy.*
> *I believe Icarus was not failing as he fell,*
> *but just coming to the end of his triumph."*

(Jack Gilbert, *Failing and Flying*, Poets.org, accessed March 17, 2022, https://poets.org/poem/failing-and-flying.)

7. Jenkins, *What Love is and What it Could Be,* 94.

8. Haag, *Marriage Confidential*, xiii.

9. Katie Heaney, "What is it Like Being a Relationship Anarchist?" *New York Magazine*, October 23, 2018, accessed April 6, 2022, https://www.thecut.com/2018/10/what-does-relationship-anarchy-mean.html. Heaney observes, "What those relationships might look like may vary greatly from pair to pair, but there are several core values shared by most relationship anarchists: being non-hierarchical (i.e., they don't rank their romantic partner[s] as necessarily more important than their friends); anti-prescriptionist (i.e., there are no built-in prescriptions about what a partnership must look like) and often, non-monogamous. (Some relationship anarchists are polyamorous, and some poly people practice relationship hierarchy, but the two are more like overlapping circles than synonyms.)"

10. This menu is adapted from the criteria created in this paper but relies heavily on others work. For example:

- Melissa A. Febello, "2020 Broke All the Relationship Rules — Relationship Anarchy Could Mend It Back," *Greatist*, accessed April 14, 2022, https://greatist.com/connect/relationship-anarchy.

- Sophie K. Rosa, "Can Relationship Anarchy Create a World Without Heartbreak?" *Aeon*, accessed April 14, 2022, https://aeon.co/ideas/can-relationship-anarchy-create-a-world-without-heartbreak.

- Amelia Lichtenberg, "What is Relationship Anarchy?," *AmeliaLichtenber.com* (blog), accessed April 14, 2022, https://www.amelialichtenberg.com/relationshipanarchy.

11. Brené Brown, "Clear is Kind. Unclear is Unkind.," *BreneBrown.com* (blog), accessed May 17, 2022, https://brenebrown.com/articles/2018/10/15/clear-is-kind-unclear-is-unkind.

12. Ibid.

Chapter 7: Neither Animals nor Angels

1. Recent research in the *Journal of Adolescent Health* indicates that "teens today are less likely to be taught about critical sex education topics compared to 25 years ago." (Beth Elwood, "Only Half Of US Adolescents Receive Adequate Sex Education — And Black And Hispanic Youth are Especially Left Behind," *PsyPost*, accessed March 20, 2022, https://www.psypost.org/2022/03/only-half-of-us-adolescents-receive-adequate-sex-education-and-black-and-hispanic-youth-are-especially-left-behind-62664).

2. I am indebted to a sermon by John Ortberg in which he laid out this continuum as a framework to think about human sexuality.

3. Christopher Ryan, "Sexual Repression: Adultery Causes Earthquakes? Sexual Repression Can Cause Much Worse," Psychology Today, accessed April 12, 2022, https://www.psychologytoday.com/us/blog/sex-dawn/201004/sexual-repression.

4. Cathleen Falsani, *The God Factor: Inside the Spiritual Lives of Public People* (New York: Farrar, Straus, and Giroux, 2006).

5. The popularity of these "rules" come from the ABC sitcom "8 Simple Rules", but the premise was derived from the book by W. Bruce Cameron, *8 Simples Rules for Dating My Teenage Daughter* (New York: Workman Publishing, 2001). I am embarrassed to say that I have used these rules unironically in sermons in my past. I got a cheap laugh from them but it was not well received by my oldest daughter who was a teenager at the time.

6. J.H. Kim, W.S. Tam, and P. Muennig, "Sociodemographic Correlates of Sexlessness Among American Adults and Associations with Self-Reported Happiness Levels: Evidence from the U.S. General Social Survey," *Archives of Sexual Behavior* 46, no. 8, (2017): 2403–15, https://doi.org/10.1007/s10508-017-0968-7.

7. Esther Perel, *The State of Affairs: Rethinking Infidelity* (New York: Harper Collins, 2017), 221.

8. Dagmar Herzog, *Sex in Crisis: The New Sexual Revolution and the Future of American Politics* (New York: Basic Books, 2008), 3.

9. Perel, *The State of Affairs*, 219.

10. "The Simpsons, 1989," Quotes, accessed May 30, 2022, https://www.quotes.net/mquote/922447.

11. This concept is outlined in Stephen Mitchell, *Can Love Last?: The Fate of Romance Over Time* (New York: W.W. Norton, 2002).

12. Esther Perel, *Mating in Captivity: Unlocking Erotic Intelligence* (New York: Harper, 2007), 5.

13. Haag, *Marriage Confidential*, 190.

14. As quoted in Perel, *The State of Affairs,* 38.

15. Dinah Birch, ed. *The Oxford Companion to English Literature: Seventh Edition* (Oxford: Oxford University Press, 2009), 691.

16. I would be remiss if I did not give recognition to the double-standard that has traditionally existed for adultery in men and women. Wednesday Martin writes that, "Along with life, liberty, and the pursuit of happiness, the sexual double standard is one of our country's foundational concepts." (Wednesday Martin, *Untrue*, 66.)

17. D.C Atkins, D.H. Baucom, and N.S. Jacobson, "Understanding Infidelity: Correlates in a National Random Sample," *Journal of Family Psychology* 15, no. 4 (2001): 735-49; M.W. Wiederman, "Extramarital Sex: Prevalence and Correlates in a National Survey," *Journal of Sex Research* 34, no. 2 (1997), 167-74.

18. Alicia M. Walker, *The Secret Life of the Cheating Wife: Power, Pragmatism, and Pleasure in Women's Infidelity* (Lanham: Lexington Books, 2018), 22 and 285.

19. Shere Hite, *Women and Love: A Cultural Revolution in Progress* (New York: Knopf, 1987).

20. Esther Perel's book, *The State of Affairs: Rethinking Infidelity*, does a great job at outlining these reasons in detail. A good summary of the book is her article in *The Atlantic Magazine*. She writes, "To doggedly look for marital flaws in order to understand [affairs] is an example of what's known as the 'streetlight effect': A drunk man searches for his missing keys not where he dropped them but where the light is. Human beings have a tendency to look for the truth in the places where it is easiest to search rather than the places where it's likely to be. Perhaps this explains why so many people subscribe to the symptom theory. Blaming a failed marriage is easier than grappling with our existential conundrums, our longings, our ennui. The problem is that, unlike the drunk, whose search is futile, we can always find problems in a marriage. They just may not be the right keys to unlock the meaning of the affair." (Esther Perel, "Why Happy People Cheat: A Good Marriage Is No Guarantee Against Infidelity," The Atlantic, accessed February 15, 2022, https://www.theatlantic.com/magazine/archive/2017/10/why-happy-people-cheat/537882/).

21. Perel, *The State of Affairs,* 4.

22. Haag, *Marriage Confidential,* 251.

23. Sarah Blaffer Hrdy, "Empathy, Polyandry, and the Myth of the Coy Female," in E. Sober (ed) *Conceptual Issues in Evolutionary Biology* (Cambridge, MA: MIT Press, 1994), 131-59; Meredith F. Small, *Female Choices* (Ithaca, NY: Cornell University Press, 1993), 193-95.

24. Martin, *Untrue,* 39.

25. Sari Anders, Lisa Hamilton, and Neil Watson, "Multiple Partners Are Associated with Higher Testosterone in North American Men and Women," *Hormones and Behavior* 51 (2007): 454-59.

26. Perel, *Mating in Captivity,* 19-37.

27. "Deluded Brides Believe Marriage Will Last Forever," *Express,* April 3, 2008, 23.

28. D.A. Miller, *The Novel and The Police* (Berkeley: University of California Press, 1988), 383.

29. Alfred Kinsey, *Sexual Behavior in The Human Female* (Philadelphia: Saunders, 1953), 416, 427, and 434.

30. John F. Cuber and Peggy B. Harroff, *The Significant Americans: A Study of Sexual Behavior Among the Affluent* (New York: Appleton-Century, 1965), 34.

31. Cf. Haag, *Marriage Confidential,* 240-41. Another example of this is how internet porn traffic is more prevalent in culturally and religiously conservative parts of the country. It reminds me of a section of Nadia Bolz-Weber's book in which she reflects, "In my pastoral work I've started to suspect that the more someone was exposed to religious messages about controlling their desires, avoiding sexual thoughts, and not lusting in their hearts, the less likely they are to be integrated physically, emotionally, sexually, and spiritually.", (Bolz-Weber, *Shameless,* 140).

32. Sometimes the terms, "ethical non-monogamy" and "polyamory" are used interchangeably but there is a technical difference. Ethical non-monogamy is a broader umbrella term that describes arrangements in which people have multiple consensual romantic, sexual, and/or intimate partners. Polyamory, on the other hand, literally means "many loves." The focus of polyamory is more wholistic and focused on emotional connections rather than just physical connections. So, all polyamory is ethical non-monogamy, but not all ethical non-monogamy is polyamory.

33. Amy C. Moors, Amanda N. Gesselman, and Justin R. Garcia, "Desire, Familiarity, and Engagement in Polyamory: Results from a National Sample of Single Adults in the United States," *Frontiers in Psychology* 23 (March, 2021), https://doi.org/10.3389/fpsyg.2021.619640.

34. Ibid, 253.

35. Jenkins, *What Love is and What it Could Be,* 175.

36. Thomas R. Brooks, Jennifer Shaw, Stephen Reysen, and Tracy B. Henley, "The Vices and Virtues of Consensual Non-Monogamy: A Relational Dimension Investigation," *Psychology and Sexuality* 13, no. 3 (2022): 595-609, https://doi.org/ 10.1080/19419899.2021.1897034.

37. Oord, *Pluriform Love,* 28.

Chapter 8: Blind to The Rich Possibility of Another Way of Being

1. Jamie Mackey writes, "The custom of voicing one's objections to a nuptial union became institutionalized during medieval times. It was introduced by the Catholic Church during the 12th century as a means of ensuring the legality of a union before making it official. At this time, people relied on word of mouth and individual knowledge to ascertain whether a couple was eligible to wed. Grounds for objection included factors like a party already being married to another, pre-existing vows of celibacy or commitment to the church, being underage without parental consent, or close blood relations." (Jamie Mackey, "What Happens If Someone Objects at a Wedding?," Brides, accessed September 26, 2022, https://www.brides.com/story/ wedding-guest-objects-how-to-handle#:~:text=Jason%20Lody.,or%20forever%20 hold%20your%20peace.%22.)

2. Bolz-Weber, *Shameless,* 70.

3. Bella DePaullo, *Singled Out: How Singles Are Stereotyped, Stigmatized, and Ignored, and Still Live Happily Ever After* (New York: St. Martin's Press, 2006), 7.

4. I have not talked a lot about LGBTQ+ issues or gay marriage in this book mostly because I believe that the core of the gay marriage debate is subsumed under the larger theological framework that I was constructing in this book. Specifically, gay marriage is a *form* of marriage and *forms* follow *function* in my theological understanding. The foundational issue is how marriage functions or how it embodies love. What kind of genitalia a person has or does not have is, theologically speaking, irrelevant.

5. Regina Lynn, *The Sexual Revolution 2.0: Getting Connected, Upgrading Your Sex Life, and Finding True Love—or At Least a Dinner Date—in the Internet Age* (Berkeley: Ulysses Press, 2005), 58.

6. Eric Fromm, *Escape from Freedom* (New York: Henry Holt and Company, 1969), 104.

7. During Jesus' Sermon on The Mount, he explains his relationship to Torah and to ancient traditions: "Do not think that I have come to abolish the Law or the Prophets; I have not come to abolish them but to fulfill them" (Matthew 5:17; NIV). He then speaks to the ethical implications of murder, adultery, divorce, etc. with the central ethic being love. Love, according to Jesus, is the fulfillment of the law and the prophets. Later in Matthew's Gospel, he reiterates this by saying, "'Love the Lord your God with all your heart and with all your soul and with all your mind.' This is the first and greatest commandment. And the second is like it: 'Love your neighbor as yourself.' All the Law and the Prophets hang on these two commandments" (Matthew 22:37-39; NIV).

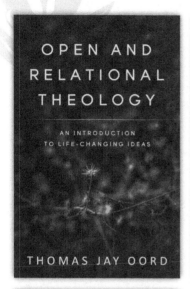

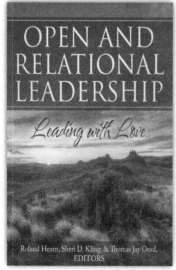
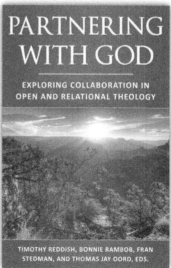

Made in the USA
Las Vegas, NV
02 November 2022

58627972R00105